Palgrave Studies in Disability and International Development

Series editors

Shaun Grech
Director of the Critical Institute
Malta

Nora Groce
University College London
London
United Kingdom

Sophie Mitra
Fordham University
New York, NY, USA

We are pleased to announce the new book series, the Palgrave Studies in Disability and International Development. With this series, we open space for innovative research, debate and critical writings aimed at pushing forward the frontiers of discourse, theory and practice. We are seeking strong new monographs reporting on empirical work, edited books, as well as shorter theoretical writings, and are especially interested in interdisciplinary offerings. We welcome unsolicited book proposals. We accept completed manuscripts, but would also be happy to hear about current research or aboutwriting projects still in-process. The series is intended to span a range of areas and we would welcome proposals on any topic related to international development and disability, including, though not limited to: Inclusive education Employment and livelihoods Social protection Disability and poverty Human rights and disability rights Health and healthcare Discrimination and exclusion Religion and spirituality Disability definition and measurement (Data and Disability) Rehabilitation and community based rehabilitation Enabling and disabling environments International development programs and their impacts on disabled people Disability cultures and identities Histories of disability Postcolonial issues Indigenous concerns Inclusive research and decolonizing approaches.

More information about this series at
http://www.springer.com/series/14633

Sophie Mitra

Disability, Health and Human Development

palgrave
macmillan

Sophie Mitra
Department of Economics
Fordham University
New York, NY
USA

Palgrave Studies in Disability and International Development
ISBN 978-1-137-53637-2 ISBN 978-1-137-53638-9 (eBook)
DOI 10.1057/978-1-137-53638-9

Library of Congress Control Number: 2017944581

Cover illustration: Pattern adapted from an Indian cotton print produced in the 19th century

Printed on acid-free paper

This Palgrave Pivot imprint is published by Springer Nature
The registered company is Nature America Inc.
The registered company address is: 1 New York Plaza, New York, NY 10004, U.S.A.

To my parents

'Sophie Mitra presents one of the most comprehensive analysis of disability to date in low resource settings. Lucidly written, this book should be essential reading for all interested in evidence informed policy and in ensuring that people with disability are not left behind in the development agenda.'

—**Somnath Chatterji**, *Team Leader, Surveys, Measurement and Analysis, Department of Information, Evidence and Research, World Health Organization.*

'Despite national and international guarantees to equal rights, research on persons with disabilities and deprivation in low income countries remains sketchy at best. In her book, Sophie Mitra addresses some of these issues and perhaps most importantly presents a conceptual framework for a new model, the human development model of disability, health and wellbeing, based on Amartya Sen's capability approach. This book is an excellent and insightful contribution to advancing the agenda for disability inclusion for policy makers and practitioners. Introducing new data, Mitra explores some challenging concepts around disability measurement, functionality, wellbeing and poverty with much needed research for low income countries and development writ large.'

—**Charlotte V. McClain-Nhlapo**, *Global Disability Advisor, The World Bank Group.*

'This pioneering book charts a way to think about the neglected causes and consequences of functional disabilities in low-income countries, and extends the concept of human development to encompass not only the returns to early child development through nutrition and preventive healthcare, but in addition the social mechanisms for coping with the deprivations due to the widespread functional disabilities of adults in the world, especially among the elderly, women and the poor.'

—**T. Paul Schultz**, *Malcolm K. Brachman Professor of Economics Emeritus, Yale University, US.*

'This book is important, refreshing and timely. In contrast to much of the writing on disability and poverty, Mitra takes a disciplined and careful empirical approach, basing her work on her contribution to theory. She charts the difficult and contested waters between a narrowly decontextualized quantitative approach and a rhetorical appeal to activist politics. It is the role of academic researchers not simply to repeat or academicise the important slogans of disability activists. Mitra succeeds admirably in providing a nuanced empirical analysis which will be of use to activists and to policy makers.'

—**Leslie Swartz**, *Distinguished Professor of Psychology, Stellenbosch University, South Africa.*

Foreword

Disability has not featured prominently on the development agenda. Despite all the talk of twin tracks and inclusive development, the reality on the ground is that disabled people have been forgotten. Investment in new schools has created inaccessible buildings, which exclude the 5% of children who are disabled. Efforts toward economic development have not taken into account the increased poverty faced by people with impairments in the poorest countries.

One of the obstacles to addressing disability in a serious and sustained way is the lack of data. Economists and policymakers reply to human rights activists that there is no evidence that including disabled people makes good financial sense. There is a world where people are talking about the UN Convention on the Rights of Persons with Disabilities, and there is a world where people are taking investment decisions, which overlook these obligations about equality of opportunity.

Sophie Mitra has long been one of the most respected and committed development economists working on disability. Her work replaces rhetoric with detailed evidence and critique. She is one of those who are filling the data gap and making it harder for policymakers to ignore the needs of people with disabilities in developing countries.

In this book, Mitra combines detailed data analysis with an interactional model of disability based on Amartya Sen's capability approach. Sen's work fits very well into the disability human rights agenda. By developing the human development model of disability, health, and wellbeing, Mitra is able to illuminate for us the complex world of disability and begins to supply the required solutions.

This short text is a much-needed contribution to the fields of development economics and disability studies. It builds on the data and analysis in the WHO/World Bank *World Report on Disability*, and helps us understand the nuances of disability and development. We need more research like this.

Tom Shakespeare
Professor of Disability Research
Norwich Medical School
University of East Anglia
Norwich, UK

Preface

This book presents new research on disability, health, and wellbeing in four countries. The primary focus is empirical. It also makes a conceptual contribution as it presents a new model of disability based on the human development and capability approach.

The audience for this book are academic researchers and policymakers interested in disability, poverty, global health, and wellbeing issues in general and in low-income countries in particular. The book can also be used as a teaching tool for students in development economics, development studies, disability studies, or global health courses.

There are other volumes dedicated to disability and international development (e.g., Grech 2015, MacLachlan and Swartz 2009, Stone 1999). This book differs from these previous efforts in that it exploits new internationally comparable data on disability in low-income countries and offers a quantitative analysis. To my knowledge, it is also the first book on disability set in the context of the human development and capability approach, where human development refers to the expansion of freedoms (Sen 1999). My aim is to offer a new way of understanding global disability issues through the capability approach and panel datasets.

The ideas and methods in this book grew out of my work on disability and wellbeing over the past 15 years.I am grateful to several valued collaborators I have learned from and enjoyed working with. First, I owe many thanks to the late Monroe Berkowitz for inspiring me to work in the field of disability when I worked for the Program for Disability Research at Rutgers University in 2002–2005. I am thankful to Debra Brucker, Patricia Findley, Nora Groce, Jill Hanass-Hancock, Todd Honeycutt, Douglas Kruse, Ilionor Louis, Subha Mani, Suguru Mizunoya, Daniel Mont, Michael Palmer, Aleksandra Posarac, and Usha Sambamoorthi. I am deeply grateful to Fordham University for financial support. I thank Hoolda Kim for excellent research assistance with data. Shannon Kelsh, Shannon Pullaro and Andrew Seger also very skillfully helped with initial stages.

I had the opportunity to present different parts of the book manuscript and related results at the United Nations Department of Economic and Social Affairs, the 2015 and 2016 Annual Conferences of the Human Development and Capability Association, at Fordham University, Kolkata Institute of Development Studies, St Gallen University and the World Bank. Comments and questions received by participants on each of these occasions helped refine the analysis presented here. I am also very grateful for comments on the entire draft from Somnath Chatterji, James English, Jill Hanass-Hancock, Nora Groce, Daniel Mont, Julius Omona and Tom Shakespeare, and on drafts of selected chapters from Barbara Altman, Vandana Chaudhry, Kim Hopper, Eileen McGinn, Gerald Oriol Jr and Jean-François Trani. Last, but not least, I am grateful to Richard Mukaga who shared his life story to provide examples for several points made in this book.

I personally thank Joydeep, Leela, Alain and Neel for their love, support, joy, and patience.

New York, USA Sophie Mitra

References

Grech, S. (2015). Disability and poverty in the global South. Renegotiating development in Guatemala. London: Palgrave Macmillan.

MacLachlan, M. and L. Swartz (eds) (2009). Disability and international development: Towards inclusive global health. New York: Springer.

Stone, E. (ed) (1999). Disability and Development: Learning from action and research on disability in the majority world. Leeds: The Disability Press.

Sen, A.K. (1999). Development as Freedom. New York: Alfred A. Knopf.

Contents

Abbreviations

CRPD	Convention on the Rights of Persons with Disabilities
GNI	Gross National Income
HDI	Human Development Index
HIC	High Income Country
ICD	International Classification of Diseases
ICF	International Classification of Functioning, Disability and Health
LIC	Low-Income Country
LMIC	Low- and Middle-Income Country
LSMS	Living Standard Measurement Study
OLS	Ordinary Least Squares
PPP	Purchasing Power Parity
PSNP	Productive Safety Net Program (Ethiopia)
SAGE	Social Assistance Grant for Empowerment (Uganda)
SDG	Sustainable Development Goal
SF12	Short Form Survey with 12 questions
UK	United Kingdom
UNESCO	United Nations Educational, Scientific and Cultural Organization
WHO	World Health Organization
WHS	World Health Survey

List of Figures

List of Tables

List of Boxes

CHAPTER 1

Introduction

Abstract In low-income countries, there has been very little research on disability and its link to deprivations. Much of the research is recent, and research using traditional poverty indicators (e.g., consumption expenditures) paints an unclear picture on the association between disability and deprivations. This is important as the prevalence of health conditions and impairments is expected to rise with an increasing life expectancy and as more policies try to address deprivations in relation to disability. This book asks the following: How should disability be defined to analyze and inform policies related to wellbeing? What is the prevalence of functional difficulties? What inequalities are associated with functional difficulties? What are the economic consequences of functional difficulties? The empirical work is focused on Ethiopia, Malawi, Tanzania, and Uganda.

Keywords Disability · Functional difficulties · Poverty · Low-income countries · Africa

JEL I1 · I3 · O15

In December 2016, the United Nations Educational, Scientific and Cultural Organization (UNESCO) published the profile of Richard Mukaga, one of six children raised by his single mother in the rural Namaingo District in Eastern Uganda where polio left him unable to

S. Mitra, *Disability, Health and Human Development*,
Palgrave Studies in Disability and International Development,
DOI 10.1057/978-1-137-53638-9_1

walk from age six.[1] In June 2016, The Guardian newspaper started a series of online articles on disability rights. Many were about the challenges faced by persons with disabilities in low- and middle-income countries (LMICs). It described them as being marginalized in their communities, excluded from work and among 'the poorest of the poor.'[2]

This recent attention to disability is welcome from the perspective of the field of international development where disability has been a marginal issue. It is barely mentioned in landmark policy documents (World Bank 2006, 2017) and in textbooks (e.g. de Janvry and Sadoulet 2016). Governments in LMICs and international donors in high-income countries (HICs) rarely pay attention to it. The term 'disability' itself is unclear and conceptually elusive. What does it mean exactly? Isn't it a subjective notion? If it is, how can it be studied and measured so as to inform policy? Internationally comparable data has been missing on disability, making it difficult to investigate the significance of the phenomenon. There is also the common perception that disability is an issue that has more relevance in HICs where, due to aging and better survival chances in case of injuries or health conditions, people's lives are extended and may thus experience disability. This perception is also entertained by the presence in HICs of social safety net programs such as disability insurance programs, often criticized for the potential disincentive to work and poverty traps they might create for persons with disabilities.

How does Richard live in a low-income country (LIC)? In a setting where most people are poor and there is little in terms of a social safety net, are deprivations more acute and more common for persons with disabilities or is disability not so relevant?

In this book, I present new research on disability and wellbeing in four LICs: Ethiopia, Malawi, Tanzania, and Uganda. This book analyzes four large longitudinal household survey datasets in Africa collected as part of the Living Standard Measure Study. These datasets have the Washington Group short set of questions on disability (Altman 2016). This set of questions identifies six functional or basic activity difficulties (functional difficulties for short): seeing, hearing, walking, concentrating/remembering, selfcare, and communicating. For instance, for seeing, it asks if, due to a physical, mental, or emotional health condition, individuals experience any difficulty seeing even when wearing glasses.

1.1 Motivation

This research is motivated by three main factors. First of all, there is very little research on disability in the context of LMICs, and LICs in particular. Much of the research is from the last decade or so. The seminal World Report of Disability (WHO-World Bank 2011) contributed some internationally comparable prevalence and situational analyses in 59 countries, including in some LICs. It showed that disability is not rare and is associated with lower educational attainment, lower employment rates, and limited access to health services. Some recent research in LMICs has consistently found that disability is associated with a higher likelihood of experiencing simultaneous multiple deprivations (multidimensional poverty) (Hanass-Hancock and McKensie 2017; Mitra et al. 2013; Trani and Cunning 2013; Trani et al. 2015, 2016). In contrast, some research using traditional poverty indicators (consumption expenditures and asset ownership) paints a mixed picture (Filmer 2008; Mitra et al. 2013; Trani and Loeb 2010).

Second, the prevalence of health conditions and impairments is likely going to increase in LMICs in the near future. Aging is on the rise because of epidemiological transitions, including increased life expectancy due to a reduction in mortality from parasitic and other infections (WHO 2016). At the same time, chronic and degenerative diseases (e.g. cardiovascular diseases) are becoming more common. People may survive conditions once fatal as the quality and accessibility of treatments and healthcare improve (HIV/AIDS). Hence, there is a need to study disability in LMICs.

Third, in the past decade, disability has received more attention in policies and programs worldwide and more knowledge is required to inform them. As of January 2017, 172 countries have signaled their commitment to protect the rights of persons with disabilities with the ratification of the Convention on the Rights of Persons with Disabilities (CRPD) a decade after its adoption (United Nations 2006, 2016). Disability also explicitly features in the sustainable development goals (SDGs) of the Agenda 2030 (UNDP 2016b). In LICs, there are numerous advocates who work toward the empowerment of persons with disabilities and they tend to work in NGOs or disabled people organizations. For policies and programs in LICs, more knowledge is needed on topics as basic as the prevalence of functional difficulties and their association with wellbeing inequalities.

1.2 Research Questions and Scope of the Book

This book presents an empirical analysis of disability and wellbeing in Ethiopia, Malawi, Tanzania, and Uganda. In resource-poor settings, the specific research questions addressed in this book are as follows:

1. How should disability be defined to analyze and inform policies related to wellbeing?
2. What is the prevalence of functional difficulties?
3. What inequalities are associated with functional difficulties?
4. What are the economic consequences of functional difficulties?

The analysis in this book is quantitative and limited to the analysis of large-scale household survey datasets. While other methodological approaches such as qualitative and/or participatory approaches are beyond the scope of this book, I do believe that these other approaches involving multiple stakeholders may assist in developing a deep understanding of issues around wellbeing and disability and complement the research in this book. Stakeholders include, of course, persons with disabilities who can contribute their expertise from lived experience. They could also include other stakeholders depending on the particular issue under study, including family members, community leaders, employers, service providers (e.g., social workers), policymakers, and advocates. This book does not attempt to cover the field comprehensively, nor does it provide a full account on disability, health and wellbeing in Ethiopia, Malawi, Tanzania, and Uganda. I do not cover important areas such as education, transition from school to work, and noneconomic aspects of wellbeing such as social relations. It does not cover the long-term dynamics of disability and wellbeing, as individuals are followed over a period of only two years.

1.3 Book Overview

The second chapter provides the conceptual framework of the book, the human development model of disability, health, and wellbeing. It is based on the capability approach of Amartya Sen. The human development model highlights, in relation to wellbeing, the roles of resources, conversion functions, and agency. It uses capabilities (practical opportunities) and/or functionings (achievements) as the metric for wellbeing. Impairments and health conditions are considered as determined by, and influencing, wellbeing. I believe the model generates insights for this book and research and policy on wellbeing, disability, and health.

Chapter 3 introduces the empirical context of this study, from measurement to data and country contexts. This book uses nationally representative Living Standard Measurement Study datasets for Ethiopia, Malawi, Tanzania, and Uganda, which include six questions on functional difficulties. The four countries under study have ratified the CRPD with Disabilities and adopted national policies or legislations on disability.

Chapter 4 through 6 present the empirical analysis and results of the book. These chapters have sections covering the literature review, methods, results/discussion, and a summary of results. The methods sections are quantitative, and not all readers will have the inclination to read them. I have included statistical methods primarily in boxes that some readers may want to consult.

Chapter 4 presents results regarding the prevalence of six functional difficulties (seeing, hearing, walking, concentrating, selfcare and communication) overall and by functional difficulty type, severity, age at onset, age, sex, and socioeconomic status. It presents results on the use of assistive devices and healthcare services among persons with functional difficulties.

Chapter 5 focuses on inequalities that are associated with functional difficulties at a given point in time. Inequalities are considered for educational attainment, morbidity, work, household material wellbeing and economic security. Inequalities are also analyzed through multidimensional poverty measures.

Chapter 6 investigates three separate issues on the dynamics of functional difficulties and inequalities. It compares the wellbeing of persons with different trajectories in terms of functional difficulties; for instance, how do persons with persistent functional difficulties fare compared to persons with temporary difficulties? It also assesses if changes in functional difficulties are associated with changes in employment outcomes and assets/living conditions. It analyzes if functional difficulties are correlated with mortality in the short run.

The last chapter presents concluding remarks that summarize the main results and derive implications for policy and future research. It does not have all the nuances of the main text of each chapter and should be read with this in mind. Overall, it shows that disability needs to be considered from multiple angles including aging, gender, health, and poverty. This book concludes that disability policies are unlikely to be conducive to human development for all if they *exclusively* use an oppressed minority group approach and focus on barrier removal. It makes a call for inclusion ***and*** prevention interventions as solutions to the deprivations associated with impairments and health conditions.

Notes

1. http://www.unesco.org/new/en/education/resources/online-materials/single-view/news/disability_education_and_work_a_life_spent_fighting_for/.
2. 'Mexico City from a wheelchair: There is no second chance from these streets' The Guardian Resilient Cities for the 21st century. Accessed on 23 June 2016 at: https://www.theguardian.com/cities/2016/jun/23/mexico-city-wheelchair-users-disability-street-workout-athlete-abraham-plaza.

References

Altman, B. M. (Ed.). (2016). *International measurement of disability: Purpose, method and application, the work of the Washington group*. Social indicators research series 61. Switzerland: Springer.

De Janvry, A., & Sadoulet, E. (2016). *Development economics: Theory and practice*. London: Routledge.

Filmer, D. (2008). Disability, poverty and schooling in developing countries: Results from 14 household surveys. *The World Bank Economic Review, 22*(1), 141–163.

Hanass-Hancock, J., & McKensie, T. (2017). People with disabilities and income related social protection measures in South Africa: Where is the gap? *African Journal of Disability*. In press.

Mitra, S., Posarac, A. and Vick, B. (2013). Disability and Poverty in Developing Countries: A Multidimensional Study. *World Development* Vol. 41; pp.1–18.

Trani, J. F., & Canning, T. I. (2013). Child poverty in an emergency and conflict context: A multidimensional profile and an identification of the poorest children in Western Darfur. *World Development, 48*, 48–70.

Trani, J., & Loeb, M. (2010). Poverty and disability: A vicious circle? Evidence from Afghanistan and Zambia. *Journal of International Development, 24*(1), S19–S52.

Trani, J., Bakhshi, P., Myer Tlapek, S., Lopez, D., & Gall, F. (2015). Disability and poverty in Morocco and Tunisia: A multidimensional approach. *Journal of Human Development and Capabilities, 16*(4), 518–548.

Trani, J., Kuhlberg, J., Cannings, T., & Chakkal, D. (2016). Multidimensional poverty in Afghanistan: Who are the poorest of the poor? *Oxford Development Studies,* 44(2), 220–245.

WHO-World Bank. (2011). *World report on disability.* Geneva: World Health Organization.

World Bank. (2006). *World development report 2006: Equity and development.* Washington, DC: World Bank.

World Bank. (2017). *Monitoring global poverty: Report of the commission on global poverty.* Washington, DC: World Bank.

United Nations. (2006). *Convention on the rights of persons with disabilities.* Accessed January 3, 2017, from https://www.un.org/development/desa/disabilities/convention-on-the-rights-of-persons-with-disabilities.html.

United Nations. (2016). *UN enable newsletter,* December. Accessed January 3, 2017, from www.un.org/disabilities.

CHAPTER 2

The Human Development Model of Disability, Health and Wellbeing

Abstract This chapter sets the conceptual framework for the book. It introduces a new model, the human development model of disability, health and wellbeing, based on Amartya Sen's capability approach. Disability is defined as a deprivation in terms of functioning and/or capability among persons with health conditions and/or impairments. The human development model highlights in relation to wellbeing the roles of resources, conversion functions, agency, and it uses capabilities and/or functionings as metric for wellbeing. It does not consider impairments/health conditions as individual characteristics; instead, they are themselves determined by resources, structural factors, and personal characteristics, and thus the model is informed by the socioeconomic determinants of health literature. This chapter also compares the human development model to the main disability models used in the literature.

Keywords Disability model · Capability approach · Human development model · ICF · Medical model · Social model

JEL I1 · I3 · O15

The notion of disability is enigmatic, even confusing. The term itself 'disability' has negative connotations, which is no surprise given the prefix 'dis' meaning 'absence' or 'negation'. Beyond the everyday semantic

S. Mitra, *Disability, Health and Human Development*,
Palgrave Studies in Disability and International Development,
DOI 10.1057/978-1-137-53638-9_2

muddle around the term 'disability', how it is conceptually defined is also challenging. Researchers have long wrestled with the definition, which is important. This chapter develops a conceptual framework for disability based on Amartya Sen's capability approach. I call this framework the human development model of disability, health, and wellbeing.

Any discussion of disability or analysis of data on disability is based on one or more models of disability, whether explicitly or implicitly. A model is a conceptual tool that helps make sense of a complex reality and tries to offer a map of the relationships between concepts. It tries to explain and describe a complex phenomenon as part of a coherent framework. A model also clarifies terminology to promote a consistent use. How disability is modeled influences our understanding of its determinants, consequences and how it is measured, and what data is thus relevant. It also influences disability-related policies and programs, how they are designed and operationalized. It also shapes how we respond to people with disabilities, whether family or strangers, in everyday interactions. For the conceptual definition of disability, there is not a universally agreed upon model. There are many models that are currently in use and the differences among them feed lively debates. Several scholars have recently argued that available models have all been developed in, and for, the context of HICs (e.g., Anand 2016).

The human development model proposed in this chapter attempts to address some of the limitations of existing models and is particularly relevant for resource-poor settings. Each model provides a particular lens on disability. In this chapter, I argue that it provides breadth and depth relative to other models: breadth through the range of factors that can affect health conditions, impairments and disabilities, and a broad range of consequences and depth through a consideration of agency, capabilities, resources and conversion factors.

This chapter starts by presenting the capability approach and its applications to disability. I then present the human development model. I later compare it to the main disability models used in the literature.

2.1 The Capability Approach and Disability

Martha Nussbaum and Amartya Sen are the two original architects of the capability approach, extended and applied in the past two decades by many scholars in a variety of disciplines to deal with a wide range of issues, poverty, and justice in particular. Sen's capability approach was developed as a framework to analyze different concepts in welfare economics including the standard of living, wellbeing, and poverty. Taking the case of the standard of living, it is traditionally measured through the ability to buy commodities. Sen argues that the standard of living encompasses more than this. Under the capability approach, Sen focuses on the type of life that people are able to live, i.e., on their practical opportunities, called capabilities, and on their achievements, called functionings. Sen has used the example of two women starving to contrast the two terms: both women have the same functioning (not being well nourished) but very different capabilities. One has the capability to be well nourished but decided to starve for religious reasons, and the other one does not, due to the inability to purchase enough food.

There has been a rapid growth of the literature on disability and the capability approach in the past decade or so. The capability approach has been used to deal with different disability-related issues by Martha Nussbaum (2006) and Amartya Sen (2009). The capability approach has been considered in how it may respond to the justice demands that may be associated with disability (Nussbaum 2006). It has been used by other scholars on a variety of issues including the philosophical grounding of human rights in relation to disability (Venkatapuram 2014), the evaluation of disability-related policies (e.g. Díaz Ruiz et al. 2015), the challenges that need to be addressed for education to be disability-inclusive (Mutanga and Walker 2015) and comparative assessments of wellbeing across disability status (Mitra et al. 2013; Trani and Cunning 2013; Trani et al. 2015, 2016).

In fact, Sen's capability approach of justice (2009) motivates comparative assessments of wellbeing that may lead to insights on the extent and nature of deprivations experienced by persons with disabilities that have implications for policies and reforms designed to remediate them and thus could be justice enhancing. This ties in with the general message of Sen (2009): 'Justice-enhancing changes or reforms demand comparative assessments, not simply an immaculate identification of '*the* just society' (or 'the just institutions')' (emphasis in original) (p. 401).

More related to this chapter, several scholars in philosophy and the social sciences have argued that Amartya Sen's capability approach can be used to define disability as capability or functioning deprivation in general (Burchardt 2004; Mitra 2006; Terzi 2009; Wolff 2009), in the context of education (Terzi 2005a, b), public policy (Trani et al. 2011a), or recovery from psychiatric disorder (Hopper 2007; Wallcraft and Hopper 2015). There is not a single interpretation of the capability approach with respect to defining disability so this brief summary simplifies some potential differences among scholars. A central idea of this literature is that with a capability approach based conceptualization, whether the individual with an impairment has a disability depends on whether his/her functionings or capabilities are restricted. An impairment is a feature of the individual that may or may not lead to a disability. Another idea is that the deprivations in terms of capabilities or functionings come from the interaction of a variety of factors (personal factors, the environment, and the impairment) and that the ability to convert resources into capabilities and functionings (conversion factors) is particularly relevant and should not be ignored.

2.2 The Human Development Model

Out of Sen's capability approach, I carve out concepts and normative statements to form the human development model of disability, health, and wellbeing (the 'human development model' for short in what follows). The objective is to provide a conceptual framework to describe and explain health conditions, impairments, disability, their causes as well as their consequences.

This model is also informed by growing evidence on the socio-economic determinants of health from social epidemiology (Marmot 2005). It also draws from the extensive literatures on the capability approach, in general (Robeyns 2005, 2016) and in particular on disability (e.g. Burchardt 2004; Mitra 2006; Terzi 2005a, b) and health (e.g. Hopper 2007; Law and Widdows 2008; Venkatapuram 2011). Of course, it also relies on the literature on disability models (e.g. Patston 2007; Shakespeare 2014; WHO 2001; Albrecht et al. 2001; Barnartt and Altman 2001; Altman 2001). Compared to earlier works on disability, health, and the capability approach, it organizes and maps existing concepts in a new way with the objective to describe and explain health deprivations, their causes and consequences on wellbeing. Unavoidably, then, this means starting from definitions and maps of foundational building blocks.

2.2.1 Key Concepts and Statements of the Human Development Model

Functionings and capabilities are the main concepts of the capability approach in general and of this model in particular. Functionings refer to achievements. 'Capabilities' do not have the everyday sense of 'ability' and instead refer to 'practical opportunities'.

Wellbeing in the capability approach includes functionings and capabilities related to one's own life. It also includes functionings from sympathies (i.e., from helping another person and feeling thus better off). Wellbeing is multidimensional, and the individual's choices and values are central.

The concept of wellbeing is closely linked to that of human development. Sen considers development to be the process that expands capabilities (Sen 1999; p. 3). This view of development is people-centered. It is referred to as ***human development***. It stands in contrast to a more common view focused on the growth of the gross national product. It was championed by Mahbub ul Haq at the United Nations Development Programme who led the Human Development Reports in the early 1990s.[1]

Health deprivations include impairments and health conditions, which are defined using WHO's definitions. An impairment is a 'problem in bodily function or structure as a significant deviation or loss' (WHO 2001). For instance, an impairment could be a significant deviation in terms of seeing. A health condition is defined broadly as per WHO (2011; p. 12)[2]: it may refer to a disease, disorder, symptom, or injury. Using the capability approach's definition of functioning, health conditions and impairments can be thought about as health functioning deprivations, health deprivations for short. The ***capability to be health condition- or impairment-free*** is also a notion that is important here.[3]

Disability is defined as a deprivation in terms of functioning(s) and/or capability(s) among persons with health deprivations. Disability results from the interaction between resources, personal and structural factors, and health deprivations. Disability identifies a specific type of deprivation or disadvantage that might be the target of policies.

Resources refer to goods, services, information owned by, or available to, the individual.

Structural constraints in the environment are included here under ***structural factors***. They include the physical environment (e.g., terrain, climate, architecture), the economic environment (e.g., markets), social attitudes, laws and institutions (e.g., home, school and work, services, systems and policies (e.g., transportation, health, and social services)), culture, products, and technology.

Personal factors (e.g. age and sex) may interact with health deprivations in the conversion of resources into wellbeing. For instance, in an environment where women are constrained in their movements outside their homes, a wheelchair will not translate into mobility for women with spinal cord injury.

Conversion functions refer to people's different abilities to convert resources (goods and services) into capabilities and functionings. They are particularly relevant for disability. For example, the same income may lead to very different capability sets for two persons—one without any health deprivation, the other one with—who both live in an environment where medical and rehabilitative care expenses are born by individuals. The affected individual has to spend a significant amount of her income on out-of-pocket health expenditures, while the former does not. Conversion could also be very different for two individuals with the same impairment in two very different environments. Converting a wheelchair into mobility is not going to be efficient in a town with dirt roads and no public transportation, compared to a town where sidewalks are paved and cut and buses are wheelchair accessible.

Human diversity: health deprivations may lead to differences in conversion factors and differences in capability sets and are thus sources of diversity. The capability approach also does not exclude persons with health deprivations from theories (Robeyns 2016) and, in fact, here they are placed at the center of the human development model.

Agency cannot be ignored. Agency is the ability to pursue valued objectives, to act and bring about change (Sen 1999; p. 19). A person without agency is 'forced, oppressed or passive' (Deneulin and Alkire 2009; p. 37). In other words, one has to consider whether an individual is able to act on behalf of what matters to him/her or what he/she 'has reason to value' (Sen 1999). This is particularly important for disability since in some contexts, there are differences in agency experienced by persons with some health conditions or impairments (e.g., severe psychiatric condition (Hopper 2007)).

Means-ends distinction: the ultimate end of the capability approach and the human development model and its applications in particular are to describe, explain, and compare people's functionings and/or capabilities. For the human development model, the focus is on how health deprivations may relate to other dimensions of wellbeing. The end of research or policy initiatives guided by this model is thus to enhance human development, i.e., to expand the functionings/capabilities of individuals with health deprivations or to expand functionings/capabilities by preventing health deprivations. It affirms flourishing as the end of human development. Resources or structural factors (e.g., healthcare services, assistive devices) and other means may be used to achieve this end but are not ends per se.

This is a normative framework.[4] It is normative in at least two ways: (i) functionings and/or capabilities are the evaluative space; and (ii) one needs to specify which functionings or capabilities reflect the values of the individuals under consideration or are relevant for a particular exercise and the criteria or reasoning used in making this specification. For example, an analytical exercise to inform policies aimed at improving school access for children with impairments may focus on capabilities or functionings related to school attendance, school progression, interactions with children in the classroom. Relevant structural factors include physical accessibility of buildings, trainings of teachers, and school fees. In contrast, an exercise focused on aging, health conditions, and retirement would obviously lead to a very different set of relevant functionings or capabilities such as access to healthcare and social participation.

2.2.2 *Examples*

To illustrate how this model works, consider the case of Richard, who had polio at the age of six. In a social policy environment where having limited mobility leads to forced institutionalization, he would have to leave behind many valued functionings to go and live in an institution. He would start a life of deprivation in terms of capabilities and functionings. In contrast, think of an environment where individuals are given supports, as needed, to continue to go to the same school and live in the same community and where there are no physical, cultural, political barriers to participation in society. If he could continue to do what he wants to do and be who he wants to be, he would not have a disability, although he has an impairment. These are two extreme and opposite cases above for the same person: a case with no deprivation and a case with deprivations.

Alternatively, it could be a mixed assessment, and it was for Richard, who remained in his community with his family but at the same time faced considerable challenges with inaccessible schools, ridicule from other children, and constrained by his family's inability to raise tuition to attend a school of choice. So in terms of family connectedness, there was no deprivation, but in terms of schooling, there was. Health deprivations may thus influence some functionings/capabilities but not others: a child could have a deprivation with respect to education but not in terms of where and with whom he can play. Disability thus encapsulates a multidimensional assessment of deprivations, and in this case, it yields a mixed assessment with deprivations in some dimensions but not in others.

Another example may help illustrate that the concept of capability is particularly relevant to disability. A given health deprivation may affect capabilities in different ways given personal and structural factors, while leading to similar functionings. For instance, two older persons with arthritis and limited mobility are not working. One has the capability to work for pay but chooses to retire so as to care for young grandchildren in a three generation household. Her children will work more and earn more after she retires. The second person, on the other hand, does not have the capability to work because based on her age and impairment, no one in her village is willing to hire her. This example illustrates situations where people with similar health deprivations attain a similar functioning (in this case, not working) from vastly different capability sets. Evaluating situations based on capability information may offer very useful insights compared to an assessment of functionings alone.

2.2.3 Terminology

While the concept of 'disability' under the human development model is important, the label 'persons with disabilities' or 'disabled people' may be problematic. It refers to persons with impairments or health conditions who are deprived in wellbeing. The dichotomous term 'disability' does not sit well with the continuous, multidimensional, and potentially heterogeneous notion of wellbeing and deprivation that this model uses to define disability. Should Richard be considered to have a disability with respect to education but not with respect to family life? The term is also potentially stigmatizing as persons with disability are by definition deprived, and it becomes impossible to convey a neutral or potentially empowering discourse around them. Perhaps paradoxically, then, I'm proposing a model that defines the concept of disability but notes the inadequacy of the term 'disability'. Later in this book, when I apply this model to an analysis of wellbeing for persons with health deprivations, I will use the precise term for the particular health deprivation under

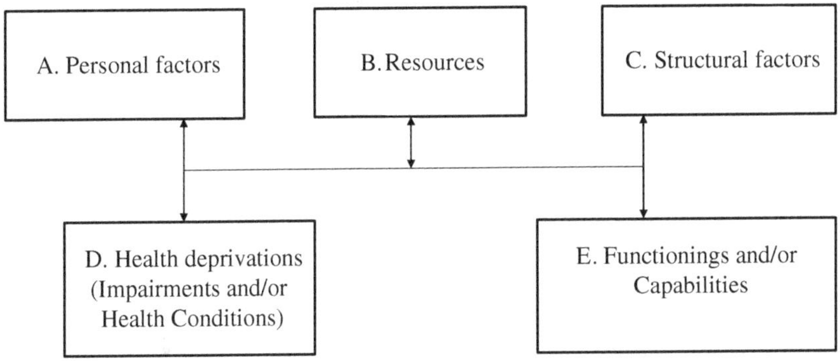

Fig. 2.1 The human development model

consideration, here functional and basic activity difficulties (functional difficulties for short). I will also refer to persons at risk of disability to refer to persons with health deprivations.

2.2.4 *Mapping*

The human development model emphasizes many potential factors that may influence wellbeing: the personal factors, the resources, and structural factors of the individual. These are represented in Fig. 2.1. Arrows describe possible bidirectional links between different components of the model. *Personal factors* in Box A are individual characteristics. They may include simple demographics such as sex, race/ethnicity, and age. They may also be more complex characteristics such as personality traits. Some are immutable (e.g., date of birth!), others are not (e.g., personal attitudes). *Resources* in Box B include goods, services, and information. They could be owned by the individual herself, or denote resources that she can access through family or community (public goods). *Structural factors* in Box C are broad and cover physical, social, economic, epidemiological, political (and more) aspects of the individual's context. Structural factors refer to characteristics of the environment of the individual: the immediate environment (e.g., family, home, and workplace), the meso-environment (the community), and the macro-environment (regional, national). At each of these levels, structural factors may influence capabilities and functionings.

Going back to the example of Richard, the human development model focuses in part on describing and explaining his capabilities and functionings and his agency. It also considers the conversion of resources, structural, and personal factors into capabilities and functionings. One would need to select the relevant wellbeing dimensions in his case to be able to analyze his situation downstream from his impairment, in other words how his impairment may affect his wellbeing.

The deprivation (or wellbeing) outcomes in Box E in Fig. 2.1 can have one or more dimensions (e.g., social inclusion, political participation, and employment). It could be a health dimension such as mortality, as long as it is different from the health deprivation(s) considered in D. One could even investigate the links between a health condition in D (say diabetes) and an impairment in E (e.g., missing limb).

In earlier analyses of the capability approach for the purpose of defining disability (Burchardt 2004; Mitra 2006; Terzi 2005a, b, 2009; Wolff 2009), the impairment was considered a given characteristic of the person that is part of the conversion factors and thus influences capabilities and functionings. This is different in the human development model which moves the analysis upstream and includes impairments as now separate and unpacked, in that they are influenced by (and may influence) personal factors, resources, structural factors and capabilities/functionings. In addition to the impairment, the model also includes health conditions, which are determined by (and may determine) resources, personal, and structural factors, and wellbeing. This recognizes the broad set of determinants of health conditions and impairments, now well-known in social epidemiology (Marmot 2005).

Going back again to the example of Richard, the human development model questions the determinants of his impairment and provides guidance in this upstream analysis. His impairment may have resulted from a variety of factors, including the extreme poverty setting he was growing up in as he contracted polio. Resources and structural factors are partly responsible for the impairment. For policy, this is useful to know as this could inform prevention interventions in poor communities.

2.2.5 *Characteristics of the Model*

This is an interactional model where wellbeing results from the interaction between the health deprivations, personal factors, resources, and the environment (structural factors). The health deprivation is a necessary, but not a sufficient, ingredient for a disability. With this definition, not all persons with impairments/health conditions experience disability but all are at risk of disability.

Of course, resources and structural factors may in some cases not be salient determinants of wellbeing outcomes. Disability may be inevitable in a given environment: for instance, given a particular health condition with no cure, the experience of pain and its effects on many dimensions of wellbeing (leisure, work) may be inevitable. Sally French, as reported by Shakespeare (2014), gives the example of a blind teacher who is not able to read nonverbal clues in interactions, hence potentially having difficulties interacting with her students. Some of the deprivations experienced by persons with health deprivations may not be able to be solved by resources or changes in the environment.

The model can be used in a static or dynamic manner. The dynamic lens is important for all components of the model, which may change over time. For instance, a particular health condition such as cancer may have subsided while leaving behind deprivations, perhaps due to the lingering consequences of treatment.

The model does not address what justice demands in terms of correction and compensation for health deprivations and other wellbeing deprivations. This model is restricted to describing and explaining links between health deprivations and wellbeing. However, results of analyses framed in the human development model can be used to demand justice. It may provide supporting materials to mobilize advocacy and policy efforts and demand justice. The model could also be used together with some of the justice claims of the capability approach in relation to disability (e.g. Terzi 2009), health (e.g. Venkatapuram 2011) or wellbeing more broadly (Sen 2009).[5]

Like the broader capability approach, the human development model is flexible and unspecified. The model is open-ended, in that not all dimensions of wellbeing may be specified. Relevant personal factors, resources, and structural factors will also vary depending on the issue under focus. For instance, if the analyst is concerned about employment as a wellbeing outcome for adults, educational attainment would be relevant as a personal factor in many settings. If on the other hand, the focus is on educational attainment, then the latter is no longer a personal factor but becomes a wellbeing outcome—an end, not a means. Unlike in the capability approach in general, this model imposes a structure by separating health deprivations, given that the goal of the model is to analyze them in relation to other aspects of wellbeing.

How does the disability phenomenon change or become any different if one moves to the human development model from another disability model? I try to answer this question below for three major disability models that have been used in social science research. I first summarize these models.

2.3 Other Disability Models

2.3.1 The Medical Model

The medical model (or individual model) considers disability as a problem of the individual that is directly caused by a disease, an injury or other health conditions, and requires prevention interventions or medical care in the form of treatment and rehabilitation. People are disabled on the basis of being unable to function as a 'normal' person does. So this model is strongly normative. In the medical model, disability refers to impairment, health condition or an ability to perform an activity in a normal way. It restricts disability to an individual phenomenon. Medical rehabilitation then has an important role to play in bringing the person back or close to the norm. The major concern of the medical model at the political level is to provide healthcare and rehabilitation services. The medical model leads to 'paternalism, pathologisation and benevolence' (Goodley 2016). For Richard, the concern under the medical model would be about his access to physical rehabilitation and medical care and his experience would justify a prevention strategy for polio.

2.3.2 The Social Model

In contrast, the social model would be focused on Richard's environment, for instance the physical environment (can he access his school?) or the social/attitudinal environment (does he get discriminated against by his teachers and classmates?). The social model sees disability as a social creation. Within this framing, disability is not the attribute of the individual, but is instead created by the social environment and thus requires social change. The terms 'impairment' and 'disability' have very different meanings with impairment referring to an individual's condition and disability referring to social disadvantage, discrimination, and exclusion.

There are several versions of the social model. UK disability activists in the Union of the Physically Impaired Against Segregation (UPIAS) developed the UK social model. Societal oppression is at the heart of this model (Oliver 1990). The core definition of the British social model comes in the UPIAS document, *Fundamental Principles of Disability*, reported in Oliver (1996; p. 22): 'In our view, it is society which disables physically impaired people. Disability is something imposed on top of our impairments by the way we are unnecessarily isolated and excluded from full participation in society.'

The minority model is another version of the social model. It was developed in North America by activists and scholars. This version says that persons with disabilities face discrimination and segregation through sensory, attitudinal, cognitive, physical and economic barriers, and their experiences are therefore perceived as similar to those of an oppressed minority group. Social inequalities by disability status are considered as similar to those encountered by other minorities based on race/ethnicity such as 'extraordinary high rates of unemployment, poverty and welfare dependency; school segregation; inadequate housing and transportation; and exclusion from many public facilities...' (Hahn 2002; p. 171).

The social model has been very influential in policy. To some extent, it has grounded human rights advances, such as the United Nations CRPD, which has guided disability laws worldwide. The social model born in HICs has recently gained prominence in LMICs. In recent years, it has certainly dominated as a conceptual framework in research at the intersection of disability and development (Coleridge 1993; Stone 1999; Turmusani 2003). For instance, using the social model, Turmusani (2003) advocates a move away from the medical model toward the social model. Disadvantages are viewed as a result of social neglect, oppression and discrimination, and thus unsurprisingly, it considers the environment as the 'focal point of action' for a policy agenda on disability (p. 146). Similarly, Amerena and Barron (2007) argue that change is needed to stop 'the exclusion of disabled people from social, economic, political and community life' (p. 19).

2.3.3 The ICF Model

There are many other models of disability, including several interactional models. One of the most influential interactional models is the International Classification of Functioning, Disability and Health (ICF) developed by the World Health Organization (WHO) and presented below.

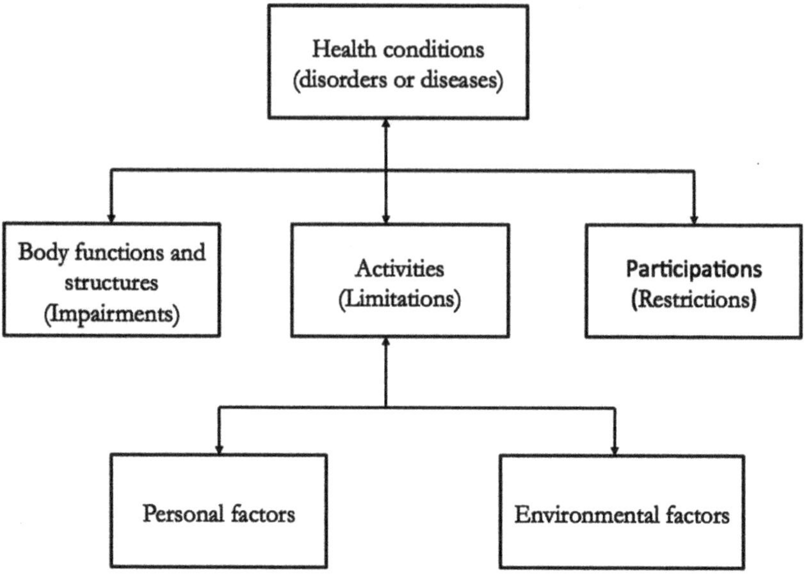

Fig. 2.2 The ICF.
Source: WHO (2001)

The ICF model was developed as a synthesis of the medical and social models to model and classify the consequences of health conditions (WHO 2001). It is a revision of the International Classification of Impairments, Disabilities and Handicaps (ICIDH) (WHO 1980). It was developed by WHO as part of its mandate to collect information about the health of populations worldwide.

Briefly, under the ICF, disability is the result of the interaction of the environment and the person with a health condition. The different components of the ICF and their interactions are shown in Fig. 2.2. This model starts with a health condition (disorder or disease) that within contextual factors gives rise to impairments, activity limitations and/or participation restrictions.

An impairment, using WHO's (2001) definition, is defined as a 'problem in bodily function or structure as a significant deviation or loss.' An activity is the execution of a task or action by an individual. Participation is understood in terms of an involvement in a life situation. Activity and participation domains include among others, learning and applying knowledge, mobility, Selfcare, education, remunerative employment, and economic self-sufficiency.

Functioning and disability are umbrella terms, one the mirror image of the other. Functioning[6] covers body functions and structures, activities, and participation, while disability refers to impairments, activity limitations, and participation restrictions. Contextual factors refer to the entire background of an individual's life. It includes personal factors: gender, age, coping styles, social background, education, profession, and behavioral patterns character. Contextual factors also include structural factors. They make up the 'physical, social and attitudinal environment in which people live and conduct their lives' (WHO 2001). They include the physical environment (terrain, climate, and architecture), social attitudes, laws and institutions (e.g., home, school and work, services, systems, and policies (e.g., transportation, health, social services)), products and technology. Structural factors may be barriers or facilitators when it comes to the individual's functioning. Disability refers to impairments, activity limitations and participation restrictions. Under the ICF, Richard had a health condition (polio), has a functional limitation (walking) and faced as a child restrictions to participation in school due to the interaction of his impairment and barriers in the environment.

The ICF has gained considerable influence globally. It is used for a variety of objectives, in descriptive as well as analytical studies and for policy (e.g., Cerniauskait et al. 2011; Resnik and Allen 2007; Okawa and Ueda 2008). The World Report on Disability advocated an adoption of the ICF (WHO-World Bank 2011). It is sometimes adopted in public health curricula and endorsed by clinical associations as a conceptual framework (e.g., APTA 2008). In medicine, it is most often used in rehabilitation settings (Nixon et al. 2011), but has also been used in other fields such as oncology (e.g. Bornbaum et al. 2013).

2.4 Comparison of the Human Development Model to Other Models

The human development model enlarges an understanding of the deprivation process (called 'disablement' in some models) by highlighting the role of resources and conversion functions, by incorporating agency, by including the determinants of health conditions/impairments and using functionings and/or capabilities as metric of wellbeing.

Resources and conversion factors are particularly important in the context of LMICs. To my knowledge, other models do not explicitly model resources.[7] Resources are not ignored in the ICF where they are considered as part of environmental factors. However, they are not as centrally placed as in the human development model where they are a stand-alone set of factors, and the diversity that may result from their conversion into wellbeing is acknowledged. In the case of Richard, growing up in poverty was a key factor shaping his life. This is explicitly considered under the human development model.

Unlike the ICF, this model incorporates determinants of health conditions and impairments: it includes them as being influenced by, and influencing, personal factors, resources, structural factors. This recognizes that health conditions and impairments may be influenced by structural factors and thus are socially created to some extent.

If this model is adopted, say to frame an intervention providing physical rehabilitation services to Richard and other persons who had polio, then the outcomes of interest will be capabilities/functionings that Richard values or 'has reason to value' (Sen 1999). Service provision is a mean toward human development, i.e., to expand relevant capabilities/functionings. The human development model thus makes the selection of relevant capabilities/functionings explicit and human flourishing as the objective of rehabilitation services. Other models, including the ICF, fall short of recognizing the importance and the challenge of selecting relevant dimensions of wellbeing.

Among the three models reviewed earlier, the ICF is the closest to the human development model. Both are interactional models with disability arising through the interaction of the individual and the environment. Both offer normative metrics. The ICF offers a metric of body functions/structures, activity and participation; it has been used and can be used for prescription, and thus offers implicitly a normative metric.

Unlike the social and medical models but like other interactional models such as the ICF, the human development model provides a comprehensive account of the variety of factors that might lead to deprivations. For instance, if a person's impairment causes constant pain, due to which the person is unable to have practical opportunities (e.g., go out of the house, work, and leisure), it is the intrinsic nature of the impairment that deprives the person of capabilities and makes her disabled. The human development model recognizes that the impairment/health condition alone can lead to a deprivation, but unlike the medical model, it does not focus on the impairment/health condition as *the* disabling factor. With the human development model, the environment alone can be disabling, but unlike the social model, it is not centered on the environment as *the* disabling factor.

2.4.1 The Human Development Model and the ICF

The ICF and the capability approach have been analyzed head-to-head in the literature (e.g., Bickenback 2014; Mitra 2014). It is thus worth comparing the human development model and the ICF. The human development and the ICF models have a number of commonalities. Starting from the obvious, the description and explanation of the disability phenomenon is central to both the ICF and the human development model; it is their common aim. There are both interactional models. Disability arises at the interaction of the individual and the environment. They both offer normative metrics.

The ICF offers a metric of body functions/structures, activity and participation, and it has been used and can be used for prescription, and thus offers implicitly a normative metric. The capability approach in general and the human development model in particular are explicitly normative in that human lives should be assessed in terms of functionings and/or capabilities.

Compared to the human development model, the ICF falls short of recognizing the importance and challenge of selecting relevant dimensions of wellbeing and that health conditions may be determined by structural factors. The ICF also falls short of incorporating several concepts such as resources and agency. The lack of an explicit and central consideration of resources can be considered a shortcoming of the ICF, especially if used for economically deprived countries, communities, groups, or individuals.

The ICF could benefit from becoming open-ended, with the recognition that not all dimensions of life may be specified and classified, and thus the classification does not, and cannot be expected to provide an exhaustive account of the lived experience of health deprivations.

Having said that, the synergies between the ICF and the human development models need to be explored further. The human development model might be useful for potential revisions of the ICF model and classification. Unlike the ICF, the human development model does not offer a classification for operationalization.

2.4.2 *Disability and Poverty Linkages*

Because of the broad set of potential factors influencing wellbeing in the human development model, policy responses to improve wellbeing may have several entry points: health deprivations (preventing health conditions and impairments, improving health in general), resources (enhancing access to goods and services), and structural factors (e.g., change of attitude or physical environment). This comes in contrast to the individual and social models, which is illustrated with the example of policy responses to the disability poverty association.

In the disability and poverty discourse, where disability typically refers to impairment and poverty refers to low income or consumption, it is often noted that disability and poverty go hand in hand and their relationship is very often portrayed as a vicious circle, especially in the LMIC context. It has become part of the reasoned wisdom. 'It is a two-way relationship—disability adds to the risk of poverty and conditions of poverty increase the risk of disability' (Elwan 1999, p. i). 'The result of the cycle of poverty and disability is that people with disabilities are usually among the poorest of the poor' (DFID 2000, p. 2). This vicious circle has been proposed and is widely accepted as the explanation for why persons with impairments are more likely to be materially poorer than the rest of the population. In the context of Fig. 2.1, this vicious circle focuses on the reinforcing links between impairments (Box D) and one functioning (low income or consumption) (Box E). The policy prescription is to break the cycle for poverty to be reduced among persons with impairments.

Which disability model is adopted to think about these disability–poverty linkages largely predetermines the course of action to break the circle. The medical model predisposes the analyst to identify ways out of the circle through preventive care and the provision of assistive technology, medical care, and rehabilitation services to persons with impairments. The social model is set to point toward changes in the environment as ways out of the circle though the removal of barriers to economic participation in the environment, for instance by changing attitudes toward disability in the community, so that persons with impairments can find jobs. Interactional models such as the ICF or the human development model may point toward a mix of medical and social interventions and go beyond the false dichotomy of having to invest in prevention or inclusion interventions.

The human development model can offer further insights. The conversion function explained above is of course very relevant here. It points toward the insufficiency of using income or assets to assess poverty.

The human development model also goes upstream by considering health conditions and impairments as themselves potentially the results of resources, personal, and structural factors. For instance, it allows for potential joint determinants of health conditions or impairments, on the one hand, and wellbeing deprivations, on the other. Low quality and expensive healthcare services may lead to impairments through a lack of adequate care. It may also lead to poverty through high out-of-pocket health expenditures pushing an individual to sell assets and leaving her/him with little for nonhealth expenditures. In this case, there is not a 'vicious circle' per se, yet some dynamic relations linking impairment and poverty on the one hand, and health services, on the other. Education may offer a way out of the poverty–disability association without again breaking a vicious circle: education may lead to socioeconomic mobility by providing a way out of income poverty while simultaneously enhancing behaviors that contribute to preventing health conditions and impairments. The human development model thus seems useful in understanding links between impairments, health conditions, and wellbeing outcomes such as material poverty that go beyond the disability–poverty vicious circle. It considers the role of other factors that may also separately be linked to impairments and income/consumption poverty (personal and structural factors, resources) and may confound the relation between disability and poverty.

2.5 Conclusion

The human development model provides a conceptual framework for organizing the links between health conditions, impairments, and wellbeing. Failure to use an interactional model such as the human development model may generate an unnecessary focus on prevention/rehabilitation through the medical model or social oppression through the social model.

The human development model highlights in relation to wellbeing the roles of resources, conversion functions, agency, and it uses capabilities and/or functionings as metric for wellbeing. It does not consider impairments/health conditions as individual attributes; instead, they are themselves determined by resources, structural factors, and personal factors and thus the model is informed by the socioeconomic determinants of health literature.

The human development model is limited to defining, and explaining links between disability, health deprivations, and wellbeing. It can be combined with justice claims from the capability approach such as the right to the capability to be healthy (Venkatapuram 2011). I use the human development model because I think it can generate useful insights for this book and research and policy on wellbeing, disability, and health deprivations. It is applied in the rest of this book using data for Ethiopia, Malawi, Tanzania, and Uganda.

Notes

1. See Qizilbash (2009) for more details on the history of the human development concept and also on the very scant literature at the intersection of human development and disability.
2. A disease is a set of dysfunction(s) in any of the body systems defined by symptomology, etiology, course and outcome, treatment response, linkage to genetic factors, and linkage to interacting environmental factors. A disorder/syndrome 'refers to common patterns seen in clinical practice which represent similar manifestations such as a typical constellation of symptoms'. A symptom/sign is the 'manifestation of a dysfunction either identifiable by the affected person or the health worker.' Injuries are 'physical damages that results when a human body is suddenly or briefly subjected to intolerable levels of energy.' WHO (2011, p. 12).
3. Some research has used the capability approach to frame the capability to be healthy in a social justice context, which is beyond the scope of this model. This literature is useful nonetheless in how it frames determinants of the capability to be healthy (Venkatapuram 2011) or health capability (Ruger 2010).
4. See Sect. 2.2 above.
5. This is consistent with a cartwheel view of the capability approach as presented by Robeyns (2016).
6. As noted in Mitra (2006), the term 'functioning' has different meanings in the ICF model and in the capability approach. In the ICF, it includes functionings that are directly related to health (body functions and structures) as well as activities and participation in a wide range of life domains (e.g., education, Selfcare, and work). Sen's concept of functionings is broader in that it includes activities and participation as well as desirable states of persons (e.g., being fit), and it can be general (e.g., being free of thirst), or specific (e.g., drinking wine).
7. Bill et al. (2004) offer a version of the social model that does account for poverty.

References

Albrecht, G. L., Seelman, K. D., & Bury, M. (Eds.). (2001). *Handbook of disability studies.* London: Sage.

Altman, B. M. (2001). Disability definitions, models, classification schemes, and applications. In Albrecht, G., K. Seelman, M. Bury (2001).

Amerena, P., & Barron, T. (Eds.). (2007). *Disability and inclusive development.* London: Leonard Cheshire International.

Anand, S. (2016). The models approach in disability scholarship: An assessment of its failings. In N. Ghosh (Ed.), *Interrogating disability in India: Theory and practice.* Dynamics of Asian development. India: Springer.

APTA. (2008). *APTA endorses World Health Organisation ICF.* American Physical Therapy Association. Available at: http://www.apta.org/Media/Releases/APTA/2008/7/8/.

Barnartt, S. N., & Altman, B. M. (Eds.). (2001). *Exploring theories and expanding methodologies: Where we are and were we need to go. Research in social science and disability* (Vol. 2). Amsterdam: JAI Elsevier science.

Bickenbach, J. E. (2014). Reconciling the capability approach and the ICF. *ALTER: European Journal of Disability Research, 8*(1), 10–23.

Bill, A., McBride, R., & Seddon, D. (2004). Perspectives on disability, poverty and technology. *Asia Pacific Disability Rehabilitation Journal, 15*(1), 12–21.

Bornbaum, C.C., Doyle, P.C., Skarakis-Doyle, E. & Theurer J.A. (2013). A critical exploration of the International Classification of Functioning, Disability, and Health (ICF) framework from the perspective of oncology: recommendations for revision. *Journal of Multidisciplinary Healthcare, 6,* 75–86.

Burchardt, T. (2004). Capabilities and disability: The capabilities framework and the social model of disability. *Disability & Society, 19*(1), 735–751.

Cerniauskaite, M., Quintas, R., Boldt, C., Raggi, A., Cieza, A., & Bickenbach, J. E.. (2011). Systematic literature review on ICF from 2001 to 2009: Its use, implementation and operationalisation. *Disability and Rehabilitation, 33*(4), 281–309.

Coleridge, P. (1993). *Disability, liberation and development.* Oxford: Oxfam.

Deneulin, S., & Alkire, S. (Eds.). (2009). *An introduction to the human development and capability approach.* London: Earthscan.

Díaz Ruiz A., Sánchez Durán, N., & Palá, A. (2015). An analysis of the intentions of a Chilean disability policy through the lens of the capability approach. *Journal of Human Development and Capabilities, 6*(4), 483–500.

DFID. (2000). *Disability, poverty and development* (Department for International Development Issues paper), UK. Accessed January 13, 2017, from http://hpod.org/pdf/Disability-poverty-and-development.pdf.

Elwan, A. (1999). *Poverty and disability: A survey of the literature* (Social Protection Discussion Paper Series, No. 9932). Washington, DC: The World Bank.

Goodley, D. (2016). *Disability studies: An interdisciplinary introduction* (2nd ed.). London: Sage.

Hahn, H. (2002). Academic debates and political advocacy: The US disability movement. In C. Barnes, M. Oliver, & L. Barton (Eds.), *Disability studies today*. Malden: Blackwell.

Hopper, K. (2007). Rethinking social recovery in Schizophrenia: What a capabilities approach might offer. *Social Science and Medicine, 65*(2007), 868–879.

Law, I., & Widdows, H. (2008). Conceptualising health: Insights from the capability approach. *healthcare Analysis, 16*(4), 303–314.

Marmot, M. (2005). Social determinants of health inequalities. *Lancet, 365*, 1099–1104.

Mitra, S. (2006). The capability approach and disability. *Journal of Disability Policy Studies, 16*(4), 236–247.

Mitra, S. (2014). The capability approach and the international classification of functionings: A response. *ALTER: The European Journal of Disability Research, 8*(10), 24–29.

Mitra, S., Posarac, A., & Vick, B. (2013). Disability and poverty in developing countries: A multidimensional study. *World Development, 41*, 1–18.

Mutanga, O., & Walker, M. (2015). Towards a disability-inclusive higher-education policy through the capabilities approach. *Journal of Human Development and Capabilities, 6*(4), 501–517.

Nixon, S., Forman, L., Hanass-Hancock, J., Mac-Seing, M., Munyanukato, N., & Myezwa, H. (2011). Rehabilitation: A crucial component in the future of HIV care and support. *African Journal of AIDS Research, 12*(2), 12–17.

Nussbaum, M. C. (2006). *Frontiers of justice. The tanner lectures on human values*. Cambridge, MA: The Belknap Press of Harvard University Press.

Okawa, Y., & Ueda, S. (2008). Implementation of the international classification of functioning, disability and health in national legislation and policy in Japan. *International Journal of Rehabilitation Research, 31*, 73–77.

Oliver, M. (1990). *The politics of disablement: A sociological approach*. New York: St. Martin's.

Oliver, M. (1996). *Understanding disability: From theory to practice*. Basingtoke: MacMillan.

Patston, P. (2007). Constructive functional diversity: A new paradigm beyond disability and impairment. *Disability and Rehabilitation, 29*(20–21), 1625–1633.

Qizilbash, M. (2009). Disability and human development. In M. Kaldor & P. Vizard (Eds.), *Arguing about the world: The work and legacy of Meghnad Desai*. London: Bloomsbury.

Resnik, L. J., & Allen, S. M. (2007). Using international classification of functioning, disability and health to understand challenges in community reintegration of injured veterans. *Journal of Rehabilitation Research and Development, 44*, 991–1006.

Robeyns, I. (2005). The capability approach: A theoretical survey. *Journal of Human Development and Capabilities, 6*(1), 93–114.

Robeyns, I. (2016). Capabilitarianism. *Journal of Human Development and Capabilities, 17*(3), 397–414.

Ruger, J. P. (2010). Health capability: Conceptualization and operationalization. *American Journal of Public Health, 100*(1), 41–49.

Sen, A. K. (1999). *Development as freedom*. New York: Alfred A. Knopf.

Sen, A. K. (2009). *The idea of justice*. Cambridge, MA: The Belknap Press of Harvard University Press.

Shakespeare, T. (2014). *Disability rights and wrongs revisited* (2nd ed.). London and New York: Routledge and Taylor & Francis.

Stone, E. (Ed.). (1999). *Disability and development: Learning from action and research on disability in the majority world*. Leeds: The Disability Press.

Terzi, L. (2005a). Beyond the dilemma of difference: The capability approach on disability and special educational needs. *Journal of Philosophy of Education, 39*(3), 443–459.

Terzi, L. (2005b). A capability perspective on impairment, disability and special needs: Towards social justice in education. *Theory and Research in Education, 3*(2), 197–223.

Terzi, L. (2009). Vagaries of natural lottery? human diversity, disability, and justice: A capability perspective. In K. Brownee & A. Cureton (Eds.), *Disability and disadvantage*. Oxford: Oxford University Press.

Trani, J.F., Kuhlberg J., Cannings T., & Chakkal, D. (2016). Multidimensional poverty in Afghanistan: Who are the poorest of the poor? *Oxford Development Studies, 44*(2), 220–445.

Trani, J. F., Bakhshi, P., Bellanca, N., Biggeri, M., & Marchetta, F. (2011). Disabilities through the capability approach lens: Implications for public policies. *ALTER: European Journal of Disability Research, 5*(3), 143–157.

Trani, J.F., & Canning, T.I. (2013). Child poverty in an emergency and conflict context: A multidimensional profile and an identification of the poorest children in Western Darfur. *World Development, 48*, 48–70.

Trani, J.F., Bakhshi, P., Myer Tlapek, S., Lopez, D., & Gall, F. (2015). Disability and poverty in Morocco and Tunisia: A multidimensional approach. *Journal of Human Development and Capabilities, 16*(4), 518–548.

Turmusani, M. (2003). *Disabled people and economic needs in the developing world: A political perspective from Jordan*. Farnham : Ashgate.

Venkatapuram, S. (2011). *Health justice: An argument from the capabilities approach*. Cambridge: Polity.

Venkatapuram, S. (2014). Mental disability, human rights and the capabilities approach: Searching for the foundations. *International Review of Psychiatry, 26*(4), 408–414.
Wallcraft, J., & Hopper, K. (2015). The capability model and the social model of mental health. In H. Spandler, J. Anderson, & B. Sapey (Eds.), *Madness, distress and the politics of disablement* (pp. 83–97). London: Polity Press.
WHO. (1980). *International classification of impairments, disabilities and handicaps.* Geneva: WHO (World Health Organization).
WHO. (2001). *The international classification of functioning, disability and health.* Geneva: World Health Organization.
WHO. (2011). *ICD-11 alpha: Content Model Reference Guide.* Geneva: WHO (World Health Organization).
WHO-World Bank. (2011). *World report on disability.* Geneva: World Health Organization.
Wolff, J. (2009). Disability among equals. In K. Brownlee & A. Cureton (Eds.), *Disability and disadvantage.* Oxford: Oxford University Press.

CHAPTER 3

Measurement, Data and Country Context

Abstract This chapter gives the empirical background to the analysis in Chapters 4, 5 and 6. It first reviews measurement issues with respect to implementing the human development model of Chapter 2. There could be different ways to put the human development model into practice depending on the objective of the exercise and the context. This chapter discusses some ways to operationalize the model and explains the health and wellbeing deprivation measures that are adopted in the rest of this book. It describes the data under use (Living Standards Measurement Study) and the demographic, socioeconomic, and policy contexts for the countries covered in the analysis: Ethiopia, Malawi, Tanzania, and Uganda.

Keywords Disability · Capability approach · Human development model · LSMS · Africa · Washington Group

JEL I1 · I3 · O15

This chapter gives the empirical background to the analysis in Chapters 4, 5, 6. It first reviews measurement issues with respect to implementing the human development model of Chapter 2. Of course, there could be different ways to operationalize the human development model depending on the objective of the exercise and the context. In Sect. 3.1 below,

S. Mitra, *Disability, Health and Human Development*,
Palgrave Studies in Disability and International Development,
DOI 10.1057/978-1-137-53638-9_3

I discuss some ways to put the model into practice and explain the measures that are adopted in the rest of this book. Section 3.2 describes the data (Living Standards Measurement Study), and Sect. 3.3 covers the contexts for the countries covered in the analysis: Ethiopia, Malawi, Tanzania, and Uganda.

3.1 Implementing the Human Development Model

To put the human development model into practice, one needs to identify persons with health conditions or impairments who experience deprivations. This can be done using a variety of methods (qualitative, quantitative, mixed, and participatory) and by different stakeholders. Assessing whether an individual with an impairment has a deprivation can be done by the individual herself, by caregivers or professionals (e.g., medical doctor, rehabilitation expert, and teacher). Of course, this assessment of functionings and how they may relate to a health deprivation is something that some may already do without the human development model. Broadly, the objective of such exercise may be to track social progress and wellbeing in general or for specific population groups: persons with impairments or health conditions in general, persons with specific impairments or conditions (e.g., blindness, HIV). Such analyses may be done at the level of a community, region, nation, or globally. Another possible objective is to understand determinants of wellbeing, whether personal, structural, or resource factors, to find ways to improve wellbeing.

This section deals with implementing the human development model described earlier in Chapter 2 through quantitative datasets such as household surveys or censuses. It presents how this book puts the human development model into practice for the purpose of an assessment conducted toward social and political purposes at the national level. It starts with a review of the methods that can be used to measure impairments/health conditions and wellbeing.

3.1.1 Measuring Health Deprivations and Wellbeing

3.1.1.1 Direct and Indirect Approaches

There are at least two ways of measuring wellbeing associated with health deprivations through survey-based data using the human development model: a direct and an indirect measurement. A direct approach asks people to report, usually in only one question, if they are limited in their capabilities (opportunities) or functionings (achievements) due to an impairment/health condition. Such an approach has in fact been used in applied disability research under questions on broad activity limitations.[1] Many countries have in their general surveys broad activity limitation questions that can be considered as direct measures of limitations in deprivations (in capabilities or functionings) due to impairments or health conditions, as reported directly by respondents. For instance, in South Africa, the General Household Survey had for several years a broad activity limitation question as follows: 'Is the person limited in his/her daily activities, at home, at work or at school, because of a long-term physical, sensory, hearing, intellectual, or psychological condition, lasting six months or more?' (Mitra 2008). This direct approach is convenient as it takes little time and space in a survey. It, however, poses two main challenges.

A direct approach operationalizes in one variable a mix of concepts (health deprivations and wellbeing) and factors (e.g., the environment) and thus does not allow the researcher to investigate the empirical relations between different concepts of the human development model.[2] Moreover, this direct approach does not provide the necessary data to monitor people's lives over time. As an example, let us use a broad activity limitation question related to schooling among children: 'is your child limited in the amount or the type of schooling you can have due to a physical, mental or emotional condition?' Such question does identify persons with perceived limited schooling opportunities due to a health condition, so it can be a way to identify children with deprivations due to health conditions. This question does not identify children with health conditions who have been able to access schooling, which is problematic. Using such a question, for example in an environment where education becomes more inclusive through the provision of accommodations in schools, one would get a decline in the prevalence of disability over time but the negative association between schooling attendance and disability would persist and perhaps worsen as people with disabilities would likely include more and more people with the more severe health conditions. This could lead to the misleading result that inclusive education is not working. It is therefore necessary to identify people with impairments or health conditions and the subset who are deprived, which is an indirect measurement.

Second, the direct measure is a subjective evaluation of the link between health conditions/impairments, on the one hand, and wellbeing, on the other. Respondents may not be aware of the ways that their health condition or impairment affects their capabilities or functionings. Responses may also be subject to different types of biases. For instance, the rationalization bias might encourage a person who does not work to report a health condition as the primary reason for non-employment, even if it is not. People may have adapted to their impairment in such a way that they no longer perceive how it affects their employment. The environment of the person could also implicitly influence this subjective evaluation: for instance, in a study of work limitation, the number of people receiving work disability insurance benefits in a person's reference group influences self-reported work limitations and explains why self-reported work limitations are higher in the Netherlands than say the USA (Van Soest et al. 2012).

An alternative approach is to separate health conditions/impairment measures from general wellbeing measures. I refer to this as an indirect or stepwise measurement. This methodology consists in empirically making the distinction between a health deprivation and other aspects of wellbeing. Some of the literature linking wellbeing and health deprivations perhaps can already be thought of as an operationalization of the human development model. For example, several studies have investigated the wellbeing of persons with mental illness (Simon et al. 2013; Mitra et al. 2013), and a growing literature assesses the multiple deprivations experienced by persons with and without functional difficulties (Mitra et al. 2013; Trani et al. 2013, 2015).[3] Some qualitative work has identified capabilities important to patients with chronic pain (Kinghorn 2010; Kinghorn et al. 2015). The ICECAP instruments measure perceived capabilities in several dimensions of wellbeing identified through participatory methods (Coast et al. 2008; Grewal et al. 2006; Al-Janabi et al. 2012). They have been shown to provide information that is complementary to a measure of health (Couzner et al. 2013; Davies et al. 2013). The ICECAP instruments measure aspects of wellbeing that may then be related to health conditions and impairments. The stepwise approach described above of assessing health conditions/impairments first, then wellbeing or deprivations has been used in the literature on the wellbeing of health minorities using the capability approach. Mitchell et al. (2016) review the findings of studies on the wellbeing of persons with psychiatric condition using a variety of methods. Kinghorn (2010)'s qualitative work was conducted so as to identify capabilities important to patients with chronic pain. These capabilities were developed into a long questionnaire, which was piloted on a separate sample and then refined (Kinghorn et al. 2015). Tellez et al. (2016) assess the wellbeing of older people with and without Alzheimer's disease from the point of view of their functionings and latent capabilities. They find that persons with Alzheimer's disease have lower levels, and a smaller set, of capabilities, when compared to persons without the disease, even when the latter have several impairments, thus demonstrating that Alzheimer's disease considerably affects wellbeing among older adults.

There are many challenges with respect to applying the human development model and more generally the capability approach, given challenges in measuring health deprivations and wellbeing. Some of these challenges are discussed below.

3.1.1.2 Measurement of Health Deprivations

To measure wellbeing for persons with health deprivations, one needs to identify health deprivations. Health measures broadly are of two types 'self-perceived and observed' (Murray and Chen 1992). Self-perceived measures give an individual's own perception of health deprivations, while observed measures rely on an external party's assessment. Both types of measures provide complementary and valuable information on health (Murray and Chen 1992). There is often no observed health data in LMICs, self-reported measures are used in this study and are therefore the focus of this section.

Health Conditions/Impairments

Some surveys ask respondents if they have specific health conditions. Health conditions may be temporary, episodic or chronic, physical or mental, life threatening or not, infectious or noncommunicable. They may be coded according to the ICD specifications for health conditions (WHO 2011) (e.g., the National Health Interview Survey in the USA). Not everyone has access to health services, which is necessary to have a diagnosis associated with a doctor/clinic visit or hospitalization. Such questions in fact identify those with a diagnosis among those who are able to access healthcare, who may be a small minority in LICs. In order to capture health conditions among those who may not have received a diagnosis, some questionnaires attempt to find if people experience

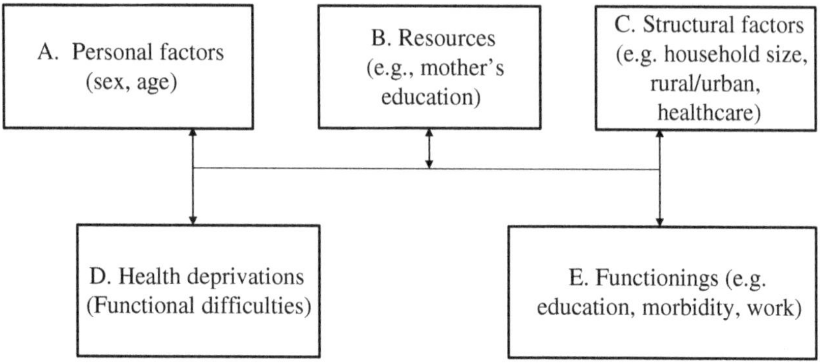

Fig. 3.1 Application of the human development model

certain symptoms and figure out if the person has specific health conditions. This is the case for instance, of depression for which a questionnaire may ask about a person's wish to die or about difficulty sleeping at night (e.g. Radloff 1977). This method may require a lot of questions and may not be feasible for all health conditions.

As for impairments, individuals may be directly queried about impairments that might include blindness, deafness, complete or partial paralysis. However, this nomenclature may be unknown or people may feel stigmatized and not self-report impairments, which will lead to underestimates (Mont 2007). They tend to capture visible and severe impairments.

Functional Difficulties

Given the challenges of measuring health conditions and impairments through household survey data, this book uses instead questions on basic activity or functional difficulties. Basic activities are basic actions such as walking or activities of daily living such as bathing or dressing. Functional difficulties refer to difficulties experienced with particular bodily functions such as seeing and hearing. In the context of the human development model, functional and basic activity difficulties (functional difficulties for short) are used here as measures of health deprivations.

Figure 3.1 illustrates the human development model as implemented in this study. It is similar to Fig. 2.1, with additional information on dimensions and indicators used for the empirical part of the study. Functional difficulties are in Box D of Fig. 3.1.

In this study, the functional difficulties measured by the Washington Group short set of questions are particular types of health deprivations that may result from health conditions or impairments in interaction with personal, resource, structural factors and capabilities/functionings.

This measure of functional difficulties is the one developed by the United Nations' Washington City Group on Disability Statistics[4] (the Washington Group thereafter) (Madans et al. 2011; Altman 2016). The Washington Group has recommended a short list of six questions to be included in household surveys or censuses. They are presented in Box 1. The questions ask about difficulties in six domains: (a) seeing, (b) hearing, (c) walking/climbing stairs, (d) concentrating or remembering things, (e) selfcare, and (f) communication. For each difficulty, individuals could respond on a scale of 1–4 as follows: 1-no difficulty, 2-some difficulty, 3-a lot of difficulty, and 4-unable to do. The Washington Group short set of questions has the advantage of brevity and international comparability. Albeit cognitively tested in 14 countries (Miller 2016), these questions on functional difficulties are not without limitations. For instance, an understanding of functional difficulties may be limited in a context with limited access to healthcare (Schneider 2016). This may lead to underreporting in the countries under study.

Box 1: Washington Group Short Set of Questions on Disability

The next questions ask about difficulties you may have doing certain activities because of a health problem.

(a) Do you have difficulty seeing even when wearing glasses?
(b) Do you have difficulty hearing even when wearing a hearing aid?
(c) Do you have difficulty walking or climbing steps?
(d) Do you have difficulty remembering or concentrating?
(e) Do you have difficulty with selfcare such as washing all over or dressing?
(f) Do you have difficulty communicating, for example understanding others or others understanding you?

For each question in (a) through (f), respondents are asked to answer one of the following: 1-no difficulty, 2-some difficulty, 3-a lot of difficulty, or 4-unable to do.

For a proxy respondent, each of the six questions starts with 'does <person> have difficulty…?'

Source http://www.washingtongroup-disability.com/

Functional difficulties can thus be thought about and measured on a continuum or spectrum from 'no difficulty' to 'unable to do'. This study uses a score as in Stewart and Ware (1992, p. 80). The *Functional Score* is the normalized *Sum* of answers (each ranging from 1 to 4) to the six questions with a minimum of six (*MinScore*) and a maximum of 24 (*MaxScore*) as follows:

$$\textit{Functional Score} = \frac{\textit{Sum} - \textit{MinScore}}{\textit{MaxScore} - \textit{MinScore}}$$

For example, if someone answers 1—no difficulty to the six difficulty questions, the sum of answers is six and the functional score is as follows:

$$\textit{Functional Score} = \frac{6-6}{24-6} = 0$$

If someone answers 1—no difficulty to the six questions except 4—unable to do for seeing, then the sum of answers is nine and the functional score is:

$$\textit{Functional Score} = \frac{9-6}{24-6} = \frac{1}{6}$$

The functional score has a minimum of 0 and a maximum of 1, and many possible values in between. Using such a score is consistent with a move toward a more plural understanding of health deprivations in general, and functional status in particular, where every individual has a score and may well change score from time to time and as part of the life course. For the household-level analysis below, the household functional score is the highest individual score among the adults in a household. With this score, every person or household is placed on a continuum.

In order to determine prevalence or identify a specific group, a threshold needs to be set on this continuum. This threshold represents a social judgment to differentiate persons with and without functional difficulties. The Washington Group recommendation uses 'a lot of difficulty' as a threshold: persons who report 'a lot of difficulty' or 'unable to do' for at least one domain are considered to have a disability.

This study uses two thresholds and a trichotomy. It groups individuals into three mutually exclusive categories of difficulties:

1. no moderate/severe functional difficulty in the six domains;
2. moderate functional difficulty (some difficulty in at least one domain and no severe difficulty);
3. severe functional difficulty (a lot of difficulty or unable to do in at least one domain).

The analysis conducted at the household level categorizes households in the same way: households with no moderate/severe functional difficulty; households with at least one adult with a moderate functional difficulty (some difficulty in at least one domain and no severe difficulty in the household); and households with at least one adult with a severe functional difficulty (a lot of difficulty or unable to do in at least one domain). Moving away from a dichotomy (limited vs not limited) toward a functional score above or a trichotomy (severe, moderate, and no difficulty) is consistent with the human development model where health deprivations are considered aspects and factors of human diversity.

3.1.2 Measuring Functionings and Capabilities

Some of the challenges in putting the human development model into practice are of course similar to those of putting the broader capability approach into practice. These have been extensively covered in the literature, from the measurement of capabilities to the selection of relevant dimensions, their weights, and thresholds for deprivations.

i. Capabilities measurement

In brief, the measurement of capabilities is very challenging since capabilities are not directly observable. So are capabilities measurable? Recently, there have been efforts to collect data on a range of capabilities for the general population (e.g., Al-Janabi et al. 2012; Anand et al. 2009), and for some particular population groups such as older people (Coast et al. 2008). In general, this literature, although at an early stage, reports encouraging results on the feasibility of measuring capabilities. This study does not have information on capabilities in the datasets under use and is therefore restricted to functionings.

ii. Selection of dimensions of wellbeing

One also needs a set of functionings (or capabilities), a method to measure them, and a threshold below which a person is considered to have a deprivation. The selection of dimensions for measures of wellbeing or deprivations at an applied level is challenging (Alkire 2007). Sen did not develop a definitive list of dimensions of what constitutes the good life.[5] Relevant capabilities have been chosen based on people's views (Coast et al. 2008) or from theory, based, for instance, on Nussbaum's list (Anand et al. 2009). Martha Nussbaum did develop a prescriptive list of 'central human capabilities'—ten ordered functions considered essential to human life and universal across all cultures based on an Aristotelian 'objective' view of 'human flourishing'.[6] This list is used to determine a social minimum in each dimension.

While operationally attractive, this approach ignores the value of asking people themselves to construct the dimensions of the good life. Nussbaum's list has led some to worry about who decides which dimensions are part of the list and on what grounds, since item selection by researchers gives the appearance of paternalism (Stewart 2001, 2005). This question of who should decide is especially salient for groups expected to have different lists of dimensions compared to the general population. This is the case, for some persons with health conditions and impairments who may require specific services or products (e.g., assistive devices, care services).

However, members of disadvantaged groups may be so deprived for specific dimensions that they are not even aware of deprivations and not likely to include them in their list. In this case, experts may then offer insights into such omitted dimensions for the group. Most of the lists of capabilities that have been proposed (e.g., Nussbaum 2000) have been developed by only one kind of expert, researchers. In the context of the capability approach, it is easy to make an argument on democratic and ethical grounds that people within relevant groups should decide, and in terms of human rights, a participatory approach engages the people who are being studied directly in research (Viswanathan et al. 2004). Furthermore, participation may be instrumentally valuable in improving the quality of the research output. Although I recognize the value of including the voices of relevant groups or individuals with disabilities, using a participatory framework to select dimensions of wellbeing is beyond the scope of this study.

This study uses for guidance the list of dimensions of wellbeing developed in the Stiglitz, Sen, and Fitoussi report (Stiglitz et al. 2009). This list has been derived through an extended and international consultative process toward developing and recommending indicators to measure economic and social progress. Stiglitz et al. (2009) recommend the following eight dimensions as constitutive parts of wellbeing: material wellbeing (income, consumption, and wealth), health, education, personal activities (including work), political voice and governance, social connections and relationships, environment (present and future) and security of an economic and physical nature.

The datasets under use in this book were combed for indicators of the wellbeing dimensions above. Due to data constraints, this book focuses on material wellbeing (consumption and assets/living conditions), health (morbidity), education, work, and economic insecurity. The datasets do not have any information on political voice and governance, social connections and relationships and the environment, which are therefore not covered in this study.

Chapter 2 defined disability as a deprivation in terms of functioning (and/or capability) among persons with health deprivations. Persons with health deprivations are at risk of disability. What aspects of disability is this study capturing then? Wellbeing deprivations are measured in different ways in Box E of Fig. 3.1. This study measures disability as a deprivation in terms of various functionings (e.g., education, work) among persons with functional difficulties. People may experience disability in one dimension of wellbeing, say education, but not in another, say work. Should they still be considered as having a disability? For precision and clarity and due to the challenges of using the term disability raised in Chapter 2, I will refer to specific deprivations (e.g., work, education, and material poverty) among persons with functional difficulties. I will not use the term disability in the empirical analysis. The term disability will, however, be used when relevant literatures and policies are analyzed, with definitions and measures as used in the reviewed studies and policies. In literature reviews in Chapters 4, 5 and 6, 'disability' will be used as an umbrella term, covering the different meanings in the literature, typically including impairments, functional difficulties, or broad activity limitations.

After selecting relevant dimensions of wellbeing, one needs a method of measurement for each of them, and a threshold below which a person is considered to have a deprivation. The threshold needs to be established in relation to a standard that accounts for the context of the particular individual. Chapter 5 will explain indicators and thresholds for each dimension. An advantage of the capability approach, as noted earlier, is to expand the evaluative space of wellbeing beyond material wellbeing and to multiple dimensions. For a broad assessment of wellbeing that accounts for simultaneous achievements or deprivations in several areas of life, one can adopt a multidimensional measure of wellbeing, or of the lack of wellbeing, i.e., a measure of multidimensional deprivations or poverty. Chapter 5 will use the method developed by Alkire and Foster (2011) for multidimensional poverty based on the capability approach.

iii. Resources, personal and structural factors

Resources, personal, and structural factors are key components of the human development model in Chapter 2. They are potential determinants of wellbeing whether the person has functional difficulties or not. Such factors could be related to functional difficulties or wellbeing. For instance, as noted in Chapter 2, personal and structural factors may interact to determine how resources may lead to capabilities or functionings. The set of relevant factors will of course vary depending on the particular capability or functioning of interest. Household survey information on resources, personal, and structural factors will be used in Chapters 4, 5, 6 to investigate correlates of functional difficulties.

Resources refer to resources available to the individual, whether purchased in the market or shared within the family or community. Access to material resources may be measured through asset ownership, living conditions and wealth, expenditures, or income. Income data is rarely available in LMICs as it can be volatile. This study has information on some material resources (e.g. assets) but they are used here as functionings (wellbeing outcomes). Information can also be considered as a resource, which is not directly captured in the datasets under use. Instead, this study uses mother's educational attainment as a proxy for information.

Personal factors are individual characteristics. They may include simple demographics such as sex, race/ethnicity, and age. They may also be more complex characteristics such as personality traits, which are not available in the surveys under use. They are important so as to capture potential intersectional disadvantages, as noted in Chapter 2. This analysis will assess how age and sex interact with functional difficulties in their association with deprivations. Information on ethnicity was not used in this study as it was not available for all four countries.

Structural factors refer to characteristics of the environment: the immediate environment (e.g., family, home, and workplace), the meso-environment (the community), and the macro-environment (regional, national). At each of these levels, the environment has cultural, economic, natural, physical, social characteristics that may influence capabilities and functionings. Information about the environment may be collected in different ways (Altman and Meltzer 2016): structural reviews that describe the environment in a town or city; self-reports of difficulties experienced by the person while interacting with the environment; and a person's participation level and how the environment at home, school or work may play a barrier and/or facilitator role in activities. Household surveys generally have few questions on the environment but potentially might sometimes be merged with other datasets with structural reviews. In the household surveys used in this study, the immediate environment of the person is known (family) and some information is available on the community (distance to healthcare services, rural vs urban).

3.2 Data

This study uses data from the Living Standards Measurement Study (LSMS). It draws on the four LSMS panel datasets that have internationally comparable functional difficulty questions: the Ethiopia Rural Socioeconomic Survey (2011/2012 and 2013/2014), the Malawi Integrated Household Survey (2010/2011 and 2012/2013), the Tanzania National Panel Survey (2010/2011 and 2012/2013), and the Uganda National Panel Survey (2009/2010, 2010/2011, 2011/2012). To my knowledge, the recent LSMS datasets collected in Ethiopia, Malawi, Tanzania, and Uganda are the first longitudinal datasets that include the recommended short questionnaire on functional difficulties of the Washington Group.

These surveys were implemented by each country's national statistics office, with technical support from the World Bank Development Economics Research Group. These datasets are nationally representative, except the Ethiopia Rural Socioeconomic Survey for 2011/2012, representative of rural areas and small towns.

In the four countries included in this study, the LSMS followed a stratified sample design with weights. For each household, one household informant responded to a questionnaire including a roster with household demographics (size number of children, age of each member of the household), questions on household economic wellbeing (e.g., expenditures, living conditions, assets). In addition, within each household, each individual or a household respondent was asked questions about each individual's education, health, disability, and labor force activities. The caregiver answered such questions on behalf of children. This study focuses on individual respondents aged 15+ as the Washington Group short set of questions was developed for this age group.

These datasets are novel in different ways. To my knowledge, these are the first longitudinal datasets that include the recommended short questionnaire on functional difficulties of the Washington Group for at least one wave.[7] They thus provide internationally comparable data on disability using a tool that has been tested in different country contexts. The Washington Group short set of questions was included in the following surveys (waves): Ethiopia Rural Socioeconomic Survey (2011/2012 and 2013/2014), the Malawi Integrated Household Survey (2010/2011), the Tanzania National Panel Survey (2010/2011), and the Uganda National Panel Survey (2009/2010, 2010/2011). I use other waves as well that do not have the Washington Group questions to investigate the association between functional difficulties and short-term mortality (the Malawi Integrated Household Survey (2012/2013), the Tanzania National Panel Survey (2012/2013), and the Uganda National Panel Survey (2011/2012)). In addition, the LSMS surveys include a wide range of indicators of economic wellbeing. For instance, it has questions on employment in farm and nonfarm enterprises, while many other datasets have detailed activities for farm or nonfarm activities, but rarely both. Finally, the datasets are internationally comparable with similar survey designs and questionnaires, and thus will be used in this study for cross-country comparisons. Despite these similarities, what people may understand from the questionnaire and how they reply could differ given different languages, cultures, and contexts in ways that researchers cannot appreciate (Grech 2016).

The response rates for these surveys were very high. One limitation though is that each survey only covers the household population in each country. They exclude the homeless and the institutionalized population (i.e., people in nursing homes, psychiatric hospitals). This is problematic as functional difficulties may affect the probability of living outside the household. Institutionalization among adults is suspected to be low in the four countries, but no data could be found to confirm this. Homelessness may be a more significant problem in its potential to affect functional difficulties.

Although the functional difficulty questions are worded the same way, there are a few differences in the questionnaires of the four countries. Ethiopia, Malawi, and Tanzania have the Washington Group questions as part of a longer health section in the questionnaire, while Uganda has a separate section titled 'disability' after the health section. Tanzania has a somewhat different answer scale including an additional category, no difficulty with assistive device as follows: 1—no difficulty, 2—no difficulty with assistive devices, 3—some difficulty, 4—a lot of difficulty, and 5—unable to do. Categories 1 and 2 were collapsed into one category (no difficulty) for comparability with other countries. Only in Ethiopia does each individual in the household consistently answer about his/her functional difficulties. In the other countries, it is either the individual or the household respondent. Finally, Ethiopia and Malawi surveys do not have the introductory sentence recommended in the Washington Group short set of questions prior to asking about functional difficulties, while Tanzania and Uganda surveys do.[8] Although these differences between surveys may seem minor, such changes in question wording or in the placement of the questions may significantly affect the resulting estimates (Mathiowetz 2001).

3.3 Country Context

The four countries under study are briefly described in this section in terms of their overall human development, their labor markets and social protection programs, and their disability laws and policies.

3.3.1 Overall Human Development

Ethiopia, Malawi, Tanzania, and Uganda are some of the poorest countries in the world. Key demographic and socioeconomic information for the four countries are presented in Table 3.1. With varying population sizes, all four countries have a young population overall, with almost half

Table 3.1 Demographic and socioeconomic indicators

	Ethiopia	*Malawi*	*Tanzania*	*Uganda*
Total population, in millions (2015)	99.4	17.2	53.5	39
Share of population under 15 (2015)	41%	45%	45%	48%
Share of population 65 and older (2015)	3%	3%	3%	2%
Share of rural population (2015)	81%	84%	68%	84%
GDP growth rate (2015)	10%	3%	7%	5%
GDP from agriculture (2015)	42%	31%	32%	25%
Employed to total (15+) population ratio (2014)	79%	77%	86%	75%
GNI per capita (2014)	$1428	$747	$2411	$1613
Life expectancy at birth (2014)	64.1	62.8	65	58.5
Mean years of schooling	2.4	4.3	5.1	5.4
Poverty headcount ratio $1.90 (PPP 2011)	33.5%	70.9%	46.6%	34.6%
Under 5 mortality (per 1000) (2015)	59	64	49	55
Health expenditures per capita (2014)	$27	$29	$52	$52
Prevalence of HIV among 15–49 (2014)	1%	10%	5%	7%
Human Development Index (HDI)	0.442	0.445	0.521	0.483
HDI country rank	174th	173th	151th	163th
Multidimensional poverty headcount	87%	56%	66%	70%

Sources United Nations Development Program country notes for the 2015 Human Development Report for GNI, Life expectancy, mean years of schooling and HDI. OPHI (2016) Country Briefings June 2016 for Multidimensional Poverty Headcount. World Bank Poverty and Equity data bank for $1.90 poverty headcount ratios. World Development Indicators database (2015) for all other indicators
Notes GNI stands for Gross National Income. $1.90 poverty headcounts are for 2010. Multidimensional poverty headcounts are for 2011 for Ethiopia and Uganda, 2013/14 for Malawi and 2010 for Tanzania

of the population under the age of 15. For Sub-Saharan Africa overall, with an expected decline in fertility and an increase in life expectancy, the share of adults in the total population, including older people is expected to increase to 72% by 2050 (UNPD 2015).

By international standards, these are economies largely reliant on agriculture. For instance, Malawi and Tanzania have about a third of their gross domestic product (GDP) coming from agriculture. Ethiopia is, among the four economies, the one growing the fastest with an annual growth rate of 10%. Ethiopia, Malawi, Tanzania, and Uganda are low-income countries[9] with gross national income (GNI) per capita ranging from a low of $747 in Malawi to a high of $2411 in Tanzania. The mean years of schooling fall between 2.4 in Ethiopia and 5.4 in Uganda, and life expectancy at birth is around 60 years. The information on GNI per capita, years of schooling and life expectancy can be considered together as part of the Human Development Index (HDI). These four countries have low HDIs and are at the bottom of the global HDI ranking conducted for 187 countries annually by UNDP (2015). Their rankings are between 151th (Tanzania) and 174th (Ethiopia). Using the international poverty line of $1.90 a day (PPP 2011), the poverty headcount ratio stands at 33.5% in Ethiopia, 70.9% in Malawi, 46.6% in Tanzania, and 34.6% in Uganda. Using the Multidimensional Poverty Index (MPI), poverty becomes even more common and affects a majority of the population in the four countries. The highest percentage of poor people using the MPI is in Ethiopia at 87.3%. Finally, by world standards, under-five mortality is high at about 60, health expenditures per capita are low between $27 and $52 and the employed to total population ratio is high at 75% or higher. The prevalence of HIV is the highest in Malawi at 10% followed by Uganda (7%), Tanzania (5%), and Ethiopia (1%). In fact, in 2012, HIV/AIDS was the leading cause of death in Malawi, Tanzania, and Uganda while lower respiratory infections were the leading cause in Ethiopia (WHO 2015). In addition to HIV, individuals face a high disease environment given widespread malnutrition, poor sanitation, a high prevalence of infectious diseases, and limited access to healthcare facilities (WHO 2015). Epidemics such as Ebola and Nodding diseases have also been experienced in recent years (Deogratius et al. 2016). The disease environment combined with stringent resource constraints is expected to have cumulative effects on survival, health deprivations, and wellbeing.

3.3.2 Labor Market and Social Protection

In all four countries, the labor market is largely informal with very limited access to formal insurance for on-the-job injuries, health, or old age. For health insurance, coverage is very limited. Uganda's National Health Insurance scheme is still in draft form (Omona 2016). Both Ethiopia and Tanzania have recently introduced community-level programs to expand health insurance coverage: Community-Based Health Insurance in Ethiopia and Community Health Fund in Tanzania. These programs are at early stages and cover only small shares of the population (United Nations 2015).

Like many countries around the world and in Africa, Ethiopia, Malawi, Tanzania, and Uganda have developed cash transfer programs in the past decade or so (World Bank 2012). Malawi, Tanzania, and Uganda have pilot cash transfer programs (Oxford Policy Management

2015; World Bank 2012). Malawi's Social Cash Transfer program is targeted at the ultra-poor and at labor constrained households (Government of Malawi 2016). Malawi also has a large Targeted Input Program aimed at improving agricultural productivity and a large-scale public works program under the Malawi Social Action Fund (UNDP 2012). A recent evaluation shows that the public works program was not effective in achieving its aim of improving food security during the 2013 lean season (Beegle et al. 2017). The Tanzania Social Action Fund has been a leading and growing policy initiative in the area of social protection since the early 2000s. Public works have been a major part of the Tanzania Social Action Fund, with further components more recently added, including a pilot conditional cash transfer program since 2010 (United Nations 2015).

Uganda started a five-year pilot project in 2010/2011, the Social Assistance Grants for Empowerment Program (SAGE), with cash transfers for older persons and vulnerable families. For the latter, vulnerability indicators include age, sex, orphanhood, and disability. The Washington Group short set of questions was used to assess disability (Schneider et al. 2011). The 15% of families in 14 districts with the highest vulnerability indicators receive SAGE (Oxford Policy Management 2015). In 2015/2016, the program for older persons was rolled out in 20 more districts, with a target of covering a total of 55 districts by 2019/2020.[10]

In Ethiopia, the Productive Safety Net Program (PSNP), started in 2005, is an integrated public works program for households with the so-called able-bodied adult laborers and an unconditional cash transfer for those unable to work due to pregnancy, illness, or disability.[11] PSNP is also linked to interventions to boost agricultural productivity. The objective of the PSNP is 'to provide transfers to the food insecure population in chronically food insecure *woredas* in a way that prevents asset depletion at the household level and creates assets at the community level' (GFDRE 2004). A recent evaluation finds that participation in the Public Works component of the PSNP has positive albeit modest effects on food security (Berhane et al. 2014). An evaluation of PSNP's targeting (Coll-Black et al. 2012) shows that in general it is targeted at worse off households based on consumption and that the cash transfer component is targeted at households with older heads, older men, and fewer younger men, and female-headed households are more likely to receive these payments.

Ethiopia, Malawi, Tanzania, and Uganda have grown their social protection systems in recent years. However, it is unclear if households that experience functional difficulties that lead to extra healthcare needs receive the necessary services or if it comes with a financial burden given limited access to health insurance. It is also unclear whether the social protection systems, with large public works programs, may be able to assist households with adults who are unable to work permanently or temporarily.

3.3.3 Disability Laws and Policies

This section describes disability laws and policies in Ethiopia, Malawi, Tanzania, and Uganda. The term 'disability' is used within the definition of the relevant law or policy, which is often as impairment or as an umbrella term as in the ICF (impairment, activity limitation, and participation restriction).

Information on the disability policy background in each country is presented in Table 3.2. All four countries aspire to improve the well-being of persons with disabilities, as signaled by several legislations and policies on disability. Each country has disability included in its Constitution, in one aspect or another, for instance with respect to anti-discrimination or resource allocation.[12] Uganda is among the first countries worldwide to ratify the CRPD when it came into force in 2008. Malawi and Tanzania followed suit soon after in 2009 and Ethiopia in 2010. The four countries also adopted national disability legislations. Malawi, Tanzania, and Uganda had their policies in place prior to the ratification of the CRPD, while Ethiopia adopted the policy two years after. Several paradigms started in HICs seem to have been embraced in these national legislations and policies. The social model of disability seems to have been very influential in the four countries with the adoption of disability definitions consistent with the one in the CRPD: 'persons who have long-term physical, mental, intellectual or sensory impairments which in interaction with various barriers may hinder their full and effective participation in society on an equal basis with others' (Article 1). For instance, in Tanzania, the Persons with Disabilities Act of 2010 uses the following definition of a person with disability: 'a person with a physical, intellectual, sensory or mental impairment and whose functional capacity is limited by encountering attitudinal, environmental and institutional barriers.' Uganda's disability policy defines it

Table 3.2 Selected national policies and legislations directly relevant to the wellbeing of adults with disabilities

	Ethiopia	*Malawi*	*Tanzania*	*Uganda*
Constitution	"The State shall, within available means, allocate resources to provide rehabilitation and assistance to the physically and mentally disabled" (Article 41.5)	"To support the disabled" and ban discrimination based on disability and other categories (Section 20)	"<…> right to work, to self education and social welfare at times of old age, sickness or disability and in other cases of incapacity. Without prejudice to those rights, the state authority shall make provisions to ensure that every person earns his livelihood"	Article 21 bans discrimination based on disability and other categories
Year of ratification of the CRPD	2010	2009	2009	2008
Disability legislation	Proclamation of the Rights to Employment for Persons with Disabilities No. 568/2008	Disability Act (2012)	Persons with Disabilities Act (2010)	Persons with Disabilities Act (2006), National Council for Disability Act (2003)
Disability policy	National Plan of Action of Persons with Disabilities (2012), National Physical Rehabilitation Strategy of Ethiopia (2011)	National Policy on Equalization of Opportunities for Persons with Disabilities (2006)	National Policy on Disability (2004)	National Policy on Disability (2006)

Sources MLSA (2012), Chilemba (2014), Government of Malawi (2006), Oyaro (2014), Shughuru (2013)
Note CRPD stands for the Convention on the Rights of Persons with Disabilities

as 'permanent' and substantial functional limitation of daily life activities caused by physical, mental, or sensory impairment and environmental barriers resulting in limited participation.'

In addition, certain strategies widely discussed and put forward in the global discourse on disability and development have also been adopted at the national level. For example, the twin-track approach (DFID 2000) of both disability-targeted and mainstream policies and programs in disability and development is part of Malawi's National Policy on the Equalization of Opportunities for Persons with Disabilities (Government of Malawi 2006) and Ethiopia's National Plan of Action for Persons with Disabilities (MLSA 2012).

Overall, in the past decade or so, the four countries under study have made great strides in developing a range of disability policies and legislations for disability inclusion well in line with the CRPD and the global discourse around disability and human rights. Of course, there may well be a gap between disability policies and legislations, on the one hand, and implementation and the reality experienced by persons with disabilities, on the other. This is a concern that some policy analysts have already expressed (e.g., for Tanzania, Aldersey and Rutherford Turnbull 2011; GIZ 2016). The next three chapters attempt to investigate this policy–reality gap by researching empirically the socioeconomic inequalities that are associated with functional difficulties.

Notes

1. Such questions have also been included in general efforts to measure well-being under the capability approach (Anand et al. 2005).
2. A similar point is made by Altman (2001) with respect to measures of Activities of Day Living or Instrumental Activities of Daily Living.
3. Mitchell et al. (2016) give a review of studies on multidimensional poverty in relation to health.
4. In June 2001, the United Nations International Seminar on the Measurement of Disability recommended that principles and standard forms for indicators of disability be developed (Altman 2016). There was a broad consensus on the need for population-based measures of disability for country use and for international comparisons. The Washington Group on Disability Statistics was formed to address this urgent need. The main purpose of the Washington Group is to promote and coordinate international cooperation in the area of disability measures. Specifically, the Washington Group has developed a short set of questions

for use in censuses and national surveys in order to inform policy on equalization of opportunities. It also has developed an extended set of questions to measure disability to be used as part of population surveys or as supplements to special surveys (Altman 2016).

5. Alkire (2002a, b) reviews several such lists including John Rawls' list of primary goods, Doyal and Gough's list of needs and Martha Nussbaum's list of capabilities.
6. Nussbaum's (2000) list includes: 1. Life: not dying prematurely. 2. Bodily health: to have good health, adequate nutrition, and shelter. 3. Bodily integrity, including physical mobility. 4. Senses, imagination, and thought: including being able to use the senses, to imagine, think and reason. 5. Emotions: including being able to have attachments to things and people outside ourselves. 6. Practical reason: including being able to form a conception of the good. 7. Affiliation: including social interactions. 8. Other species: 'Being able to live with concern for and in relation to animals, plants and the world of nature.' 9. Play: 'Being able to laugh, to play, to enjoy recreational activities.' 10. Control over one's environment. (A) Political: including political participation; (B) Material: 'Being able to hold property...; having the right to seek employment on an equal basis as others...'.
7. The Nigeria General Household Survey also includes Washington Group questions. However, it was not included in this study due to inconsistencies in age/birth year self-reports in the two waves.
8. The introductory sentence reads as follows: 'Because of a physical, mental or emotional health condition...'.
9. Income country groups are as defined by the World Bank. Available at: https://datahelpdesk.worldbank.org/knowledgebase/articles/906519.
10. For this expansion, the vulnerable families component was dropped. Only the senior citizens grant component (older persons) was rolled out.
11. I could not find from the PSNP literature how 'disability' is determined in this context.
12. In Uganda, Article 21 of the Constitution bans discrimination based on disability among other categories (gender, age, tribe). In Ethiopia, Article 415 of the Constitution is as follows: 'The State shall, within available means, allocate resources to provide rehabilitation and assistance to the physically and mentally disabled.'

References

Aldersey, H. M., & Rutherford Turnbull, H. (2011). The United Republic of Tanzania's national policy on disability: A policy analysis. *Journal of Disability Policy Studies, 22*(3), 160–169.

Al-Janabi, H., Flynn, T., & Coast, J. (2012). Development of a self-report measure of capability wellbeing for adults: The ICECAP-A. *Quality of Life Research, 21*(1), 167–176.

Alkire, S. (2002a). Dimensions of human development. *World Development, 30*(2), 181–205.

Alkire, S. (2002b). *Valuing freedoms: Sen's capability approach and poverty reduction.* Oxford: Oxford University Press.

Alkire, S. (2007). Choosing dimensions: The capability approach and multidimensional poverty. In N. Kakwanit & J. Silber (Eds.), *The many dimensions of poverty,* pp. 89–119. New York: Palgrave-MacMillan.

Alkire, S., & Foster, J. (2011). Counting and multidimensional poverty measurement. *Journal of Public Economics, 95,* 476–487.

Altman, B. M. (2001). Definitions of disability and their operationalization. In Barnartt, S. N. & Altman, B. M. (eds) (2001). *Exploring theories and expanding methodologies: where we are and were we need to go,* pp. 77–100. Research in Social Science and Disability (Vol. 2). Amsterdam: JAI Elsevier science.

Altman, B. M. (Ed.). (2016). *International measurement of disability: Purpose, method and application, the work of the Washington group.* Social indicators research series 61. Springer: Cham.

Altman, B. M., & Meltzer, H. (2016). Developing tools to identify environmental factors as context for disability: A theoretical perspective. In Altman, B. M. (Ed.). *International measurement of disability: Purpose, method and application, the work of the Washington group,* pp. 183–206. Social indicators research series 61. Springer: Cham.

Anand, P., Hunter, G., Carter, I., Dowding, K., Guala, F., & Van Hees, M. (2009). The development of capability indicators. *Journal of Human Development and Capabilities, 10*(1), 125–152.

Anand, P., Hunter, G., & Smith, R. (2005). Capabilities and wellbeing: Evidence based on the Sen-Nussbaum approach to welfare. *Social Indicators Research, 74*(1), 9–55.

Barnartt, S.N. & Altman, B.M. (eds) (2001). Exploring theories and expanding methodologies: where we are and were we need to go. Research in Social Science and Disability (Vol. 2). Amsterdam: JAI Elsevier science.

Beegle, K., Galasso, E., & Goldberg, J. (2017). *Direct and indirect effects of Malawi's public works program on food security* (Working Paper). http://econweb.umd.edu/~goldberg/docs/pwp.pdf. Accessed 27 Jan 2017.

Berhane, G., Gilligan, D. O., Hoddinott, J., Kumar, N., & Affesse, A. S. (2014). Can social protection work in Africa? The impact of Ethiopia's productive safety net programme. *Economic Development and Cultural Change, 63*(1), 1–26.

Chilemba, E. M. (2014). Malawi. In *African disability rights yearbook* (Vol. 2, pp. 207–226). Hatfield: University of Pretoria Law Press. http://www.adry.

up.ac.za/images/adry/volume2_2014/adry_2014_2_full_text.pdf. Accessed 24 July 2016.

Coast, J., Flynn, T. N., Natarajan, L., Sproston, K., Lewis, J., Louviere, J. J., et al. (2008). Valuing the ICECAP capability index for older people. *Social Science and Medicine, 67*(5), 874–882.

Coll-Black, S., Gilligan, D., Hoddinott, J., Kumar, N., Taffesse, A. S., & Wiseman, W. (2012). Targeting food security interventions in Ethiopia: The productive safety net programme. In P. Dorosh & S. Rashid (Eds.), *Food and agriculture in Ethiopia: Progress and policy challenges*. Philadelphia: University of Pennsylvania Press.

Couzner, L., Crotty, M., Norman, R., & Ratcliffe, J. (2013). A comparison of the EQ-5D-3L and ICECAP-O in an older post-acute patient population relative to the general population. *Applied Health Economics and Health Policy, 11*(4), 415–425. doi:10.1007/s40258-013-0039-8.

Davis, J. C., Liu-Ambrose, T., Richardson, C. G., & Bryan, S. (2013). A comparison of the ICECAP-O with EQ-5D in a falls prevention clinical setting: Are they complements or substitutes? *Quality of Life Research, 22*(5), 969–977. doi:10.1007/s11136-012-0225-4. Epub 2012 Jun 22.

Deogratius, M. A., David, K. L., & Christopher, O. G. (2016). The enigmatic nodding syndrome outbreak in northern Uganda: An analysis of the disease burden and national response strategies. *Health Policy and Planning, 31*(3), 285–292.

DFID (2000), Disability, Poverty and Development, Department for International Development, Issues paper, U.K. accessed on January 13, 2017: http://hpod.org/pdf/Disability-poverty-and-development.pdf.

GFDRE (Government of the Federal Democratic Republic of Ethiopia). (2004). *Productive safety net programme: Programme implementation manual*. Addis Ababa: Ministry of Agriculture and Rural Development.

GIZ. (2016). *Applied research concerning inclusion of persons with disabilities in systems of social protection*. https://blogs.lshtm.ac.uk/disabilitycentre/files/2015/08/giz2015-en-report-tanzania-policy-analysis.pdf. Accessed 24 July 2016.

Government of Malawi. (2006). *National policy on the equalization of opportunities for persons with disabilities*. Lilongwe: Ministry of Persons with Disabilities and the Elderly. https://www.medbox.org/national…equalisation-of-opportunities-for-persons-with-dis. Accessed 24 July 2016.

Government of Malawi. (2016). *Social cash transfer programme*. Ministry of Gender, Children, Disability and Social Welfare. http://www.gender.gov.mw/index.php/2013-08-19-17-29-14/social-cash-transfer-programme. Accessed 24 July 2016.

Grech, S. (2016). Disability and poverty: Complex interactions and critical reframings. In Grech, S. and Soldatic, K. (eds) (2016). *Disability in the Global*

South: the Critical Handbook, pp. 217–236 International Perspectives on Social Policy, Administration and Practice. Switzerland: Springer.

Grewal, I., Lewis, J., Flynn, T., Brown, J., Bond, J., & Coast, J. (2006). Developing attributes for a generic quality of life measure for older people: Preferences or capabilities? *Social Science & Medicine, 62*(8), 1891–1901.

Kinghorn, P. (2010). *Developing a capability approach to measure and value quality of life: Application to chronic pain.* Ph.D. thesis, School of Medicine, Health Policy and Practice, University of East Anglia.

Kinghorn, P., Robinson, A., & Smith, R. D. (2015). Developing a capability-based questionnaire as an alternative method for assessing wellbeing in patients with chronic pain. *Social Indicators Research, 120*(897), 916.

Madans, J. H., Loeb, M. E., & Altman, B. M. (2011). Measuring disability and monitoring the UN convention on the rights of persons with disabilities: The work of the Washington Group on Disability Statistics. *BMC Public Health, 11*, 1–8.

Mathiowetz, N. A. (2001). Methodological issues in the measurement of persons with disabilities. In Barnartt, S. N. & Altman, B. M. (eds) (2001). *Exploring theories and expanding methodologies: where we are and were we need to go*, pp. 125–144. Research in Social Science and Disability (Vol. 2). Amsterdam: JAI Elsevier science.

Miller, K. (2016). Summary of Washington Group question evaluation studies. pp. 69–84. In Altman, B. M. (Ed.). *International measurement of disability: Purpose, method and application, the work of the Washington group*, pp. 69–84. Social indicators research series 61. Springer: Cham.

Mitchell, P. M., Roberts, T. E., Barton, P. M., & Coast, J. (2016). Applications of the capability approach in the health field: A literature review. *Social Indicators Research*. doi:10.1007/s11205-016-1356-8.

Mitra, S. (2008). The recent decline in the employment of persons with disabilities in South Africa, 1998–2006. *South African Journal of Economics, 76*(3), 480–492.

Mitra, S., K. Jones, B. Vick, D. Brown, E. McGinn and M-J Alexander (2013). Implementing a Multi-dimensional Poverty Measure using Mixed Methods. *Social Indicators Research, 110*(3), 1061–1081.

MLSA. (2012). *National plan of action for persons with disabilities.* Addis Ababa: Ministry of Labour and Social Affairs. http://www.ilo.org/dyn/natlex/natlex4.detail?p_lang=en&p_isn=94528&p_country=ETH&p_count=141. Accessed 24 July 2014.

Mont, D. (2007). Measuring health and disability. *Lancet, 369*, 1548–1663, and Social Protection Paper 0706, World Bank.

Murray, C. J. L., & Chen, L. C. (1992). Understanding morbidity change. *Population and Development Review, 18*(3), 481–503.

Nussbaum, M. C. (2000). *Women and human development*. Cambridge: Cambridge University Press.

Omona, J. (2016) Social Policies for Inclusive and Sustainable Development: A comparison of Social Health Protection systems in Uganda and Thailand. In Musahara, H. (ed). *Inclusive Growth and Development issues in Eastern and Southern Africa*. pp. 139–173. Ethiopia: Organisation for Social Science Research in Eastern and Southern Africa (OSSREA).

OPHI (2016). Country briefings.Oxford: Oxford Poverty and Human Development Initaitive. Accessed January 2017 at: http://www.dataforall.org/dashboard/ophi/index.php/mpi/country_briefings

Oyaro, L.O. (2014) Uganda, pp. 247–266 in African Disability Rights Yearbook Vol 2 University of Pretoria Law Press. Accessed on July 24th, 2016 at: http://www.adry.up.ac.za/images/adry/volume2_2014/adry_2014_2_full_text.pdf

Oxford Policy Management. (2015). *Evaluation of the social assistance grants for empowerment programme: Impact after one year of operations 2012/13*. Oxford: Oxford Policy Management.

Radloff, L. S. (1977). The CES-D scale. *Applied Psychological Measurement, 1*(3), 385–401.

Schneider, M. (2016). Cross-national issues in disability data collection. In Altman, B. M. (Ed.). *International measurement of disability: Purpose, method and application, the work of the Washington group*, pp. 15–28. Social indicators research series 61. Springer: Cham.

Schneider, M., Waliuya, W., Munsanje, J., & Swartz, L. (2011). Reflections on including disability in social protection programmes. *IDS Bulletin, 42*(6), 38–44.

Shughuru, P. J. (2013). Tanzania. In *African disability rights yearbook* (Vol. 1, pp. 341–357). Hatfield: University of Pretoria Law Press. http://www.adry.up.ac.za/images/adry/volume1_2013/adry_2013_1_tanzania.pdf. Accessed 24 July 2016.

Simon, J., Anand, P., Gray, A., Rugsaka, J., Yeeles, K., & Burns, T. (2013). Operationalising the capability approach for outcome measurement in mental health research. *Social Science and Medicine, 98*, 187–196.

Stewart, F. (2001). Book review of women and human development by Martha Nussbaum. *Journal of International Development, 13*, 1189–1202.

Stewart, F. (2005). Groups and capabilities. *Journal of Human Development, 6*(2), 185–204.

Stewart, A., & Ware, J. (Eds.). (1992). *Measuring functioning and wellbeing*. Santa Monica: The Rand Corporation.

Stiglitz, J. E., Sen, A. K., & Fitoussi, J. P. (2009). *Report by the commission on the measurement of economic performance and social progress*. Paris: Commission on the Measurement of Economic Performance and Social Progress. Available at www.stiglitz-sen-fitoussi.fr/en/index.htm.

Tellez, J., Krishnakumar, J., Bungener, M., & Le Galès, C. (2016). Capability deprivation of people with Alzheimer's disease: An empirical analysis using a national survey. *Social Science* & *Medicine, 151*(C), 56–68.

Trani, J., Bakhshi, P., Myer Tlapek, S., Lopez, D., & Gall, F. (2015). Disability and poverty in Morocco and Tunisia: A multidimensional approach. *Journal of Human Development and Capabilities, 16*(4), 518–548.

Trani, J.F., & Canning, T.I.. (2013) Child poverty in an emergency and conflict context: *A multidimensional profile and an identification of the poorest children in Western Darfur. World Development 48*, 48–70.

UNDP. (2012). *Malawi case study: Social protection measures and labour markets* (UNDP Discussion Paper). United Nationals Development Programme.

United Nations. (2015). *Social protection in Tanzania: Establishing a national system through consolidation, coordination and reform of existing measures.* http://www.unicef.org/tanzania/Fact_sheet.pdf. Accessed 24 July 2006.

UNPD. (2015). *World population prospects, the 2015 revision.* New York: United Nations Population Division.

Van Soest, A., Andreyeva, T., Kapteyn, A., & Smith, J. P. (2012). Self reported disability and reference groups. In D. A. Wise (Ed.), *Investigations in the economics of aging* (pp. 237–264). National Bureau of Economic Research Series Working paper 17153. Chicago: University of Chicago Press.

Viswanathan, M., Ammerman, A., & Eng, E. (2004). *Community-based participatory research: Assessing the evidence* (Summary, Evidence Report/ Technology Assessment: Number 99). Rockville, MD: Agency for Healthcare Research and Quality.

WHO. (2011). *ICD-11 alpha: Content model reference guide.* Geneva: WHO.

WHO. (2015). *Country statistics and global health estimates by WHO and UN partners.* http://who.int/gho/mortality_burden_disease/en/.

World Bank. (2012). *Safety nets: Cash transfers* (Africa Policy Briefs). Human Development Africa.

CHAPTER 4

Prevalence of Functional Difficulties

Abstract This chapter estimates the prevalence of disability measured through functional difficulties. In Ethiopia, Malawi, Tanzania, and Uganda, the prevalence of functional difficulties ranges from 10.8 to 15.1%. In the four countries, the prevalence of functional difficulties at the household level ranges from one in five to one in three households. Functional difficulties disproportionately affect older individuals and women. Seeing and walking limitations are the most prevalent limitations in the four countries. A majority of individuals do not take any measure to reduce their functional difficulties, suggesting there may be scope for prevention. There is a strong socioeconomic gradient in prevalence. Prevalence is two to four times higher in households in the poorest quintile compared to the richest quintile.

Keywords Disability · Prevalence · Poverty · Gender · Aging · Africa

JEL I1 · I3 · O15

S. Mitra, *Disability, Health and Human Development*,
Palgrave Studies in Disability and International Development,
DOI 10.1057/978-1-137-53638-9_4

Policymakers in LMICs currently have very little guidance from statistics regarding the magnitude or nature of functional difficulties. Until recently, data was often not collected, or of poor quality and not comparable across countries. The Washington Group questions allow us to present nationally representative and comparable prevalence estimates.

The main goal of this chapter is to present nationally representative estimates of the prevalence of functional difficulties among adults in Ethiopia, Malawi, Tanzania, and Uganda. Finding out about prevalence is important for several reasons. It helps policymakers, analysts, and researchers understand functional status in their countries. It also helps with the design of interventions in order to prevent functional difficulties and to improve the wellbeing of persons who experience such difficulties, including health, economic, and social wellbeing.

This chapter uses data for Ethiopia, Malawi, Tanzania, and Uganda to answer several questions: how prevalent are functional difficulties? What types of functional difficulties can be found? Do people take any measure to curb their difficulties? Are functional difficulties consistently experienced overtime? What are their correlates? In the context of the human development model, this chapter measures the prevalence of one type of health deprivation (functional difficulties) and investigates its correlates with personal factors (age, sex), resources (mother's education), and structural factors (rural/urban, distance to healthcare services).

4.1 Literature on Disability Prevalence in LMICs

As of June 2016, there are a number of estimates of disability prevalence in LMICs from both country and global-level data collection efforts. Let us take the example of Ethiopia. What do we know so far about disability prevalence in this populous country of the horn of Africa? In Ethiopia, in 2007, the Census came up with a national disability prevalence of 1% (CSA 2007). This is not unusual in LMICs (WHO-World Bank 2011, Appendix 1). Like many low-income or African countries, prevalence was found to be low compared to prevalence estimates in HICs often between 15 and 20%. Is there underreporting of disability in LICs? Is there excessive mortality associated with disability? Does it reflect a very different population pyramid? Are disability measures radically different from those used in HICs? There is of course a combination of factors, but clearly measurement plays an important role in explaining the vast range of estimates across country groups. Ethiopia's 2007 Census used a single question asking if the person has 'a problem of seeing, hearing, speaking and/or standing/walking/seating, body parts movement, functioning of hands/legs or mental retardation or mental problem or mental/physical damages?'A single question asking directly about 'disability' or about impairments (e.g., mental retardation), or about a mix of impairments and functional difficulties as in the case of Ethiopia, tends to capture very extreme and permanent disabilities only and lead to very low prevalence rates (Mont 2007). Estimates using such questions are thus not comparable to those usually much higher found in HICs using several questions on functional difficulties (e.g., difficulty seeing) and activity limitations (e.g., selfcare difficulty).

Some global data initiatives have also provided estimates of prevalence for countries in LMICs. As part of the Global Burden of Disease (GBD) study (Murray and Lopez 1996), disability prevalence is inferred from data on health conditions and impairments alone using assumptions on distributions of limitations that may result from health conditions and impairments. According to the GBD study, disability prevalence in Ethiopia stands at 11.3% (WHO 2008).

Another global effort to estimate disability prevalence in LMICs (and globally) is in the World Report on Disability (WHO–World Bank 2011). It uses a score that aggregates answers to 15 questions in the World Health Survey (WHS) on difficulties experienced in eight domains (vision, mobility, cognition, selfcare, pain, interpersonal relationships, sleep and energy, affect) (WHO–World Bank 2011).[1] According to the World Report on Disability, disability prevalence in Ethiopia stands at 17.6% among adults using a standardized population structure. Using also the WHS dataset, Mitra and Sambamoorthi (2014) measure disability as having at least one severe or extreme difficulty with bodily functions (seeing) and basic activities (concentrating, moving around, selfcare). For Ethiopia, Mitra and Sambamoorthi (2014) find a disability prevalence among adults of 14.2% using a standardized population structure, and 12.7% for its actual population structure.[2,3]

This range of estimates for Ethiopia from 1 to 17.6% is potentially confusing and not helpful for policy and may curb policy and research initiatives with respect to disability. They illustrate that considerable uncertainty remains on disability prevalence, especially in LICs and in Africa in particular, where very few surveys have been conducted. To our knowledge, very few country estimates are available in Africa using the internationally comparable and tested Washington Group questions except for a few countries where estimates have become available in recent years (South Africa (Statistics South Africa 2014 and NDSD 2015); Zambia (Eide and Loeb 2006); Tanzania (NBS 2008); and Uganda (UBOS 2016). This chapter attempts to fill part of this gap for Ethiopia, Malawi, Tanzania, and Uganda using recent datasets with the Washington Group short set of questions.

4.2 Methodology

This chapter uses cross-sectional samples that are nationally representative for Malawi, Tanzania, and Uganda and representative of rural areas and small towns for Ethiopia. For Malawi and Tanzania, in each case, the only wave with the Washington Group questions is used: for Malawi, the 2010/2011 Third Integrated Household Survey and for Tanzania, the 2010/2011 National Panel Survey, respectively. For Ethiopia and Uganda, I use the initial wave of the panel dataset in which the Washington Group questions are used: the 2011/2012 wave of the Ethiopia Rural Socioeconomic Survey and the 2009/2010 wave of the Uganda National Panel Survey.

The questions on functional difficulties are as explained earlier in Chapter 3. Basic proportions are used to calculate prevalence in each country, and adjustments are made for complex sampling (clustering, strata, and weights). Although one of the objectives of this book is to make cross-country comparisons of prevalence rates, the estimates are not age and sex standardized. As seen in Chapter 3, the population structures of the four countries are somewhat similar. The objective is to present prevalence estimates for the current population structure in each country and their implications for policy, and thus the age/sex standardization is not necessary.

4.3 Prevalence at the Individual Level

Table 4.1 presents results on prevalence overall among adults and by sex and age group. Prevalence is presented for the entire adult population defined as ages 15 and over and for four age groups, overall and by sex.[4] The prevalence of moderate and severe functional difficulties (at least some difficulty in one domain) stands at 12.85% in Ethiopia, 10.78% in Malawi, 15.05% in Tanzania, and 15.36% in Uganda. Prevalence rates for severe difficulties (at least a lot of difficulty in one domain) are as

Table 4.1 Prevalence of functional difficulties by sex and age group (%)

	Ethiopia		*Malawi*		*Tanzania*		*Uganda*	
	Severe	Moderate & Severe	Severe	Moderate & Severe	Severe	Moderate & Severe	Severe	Moderate & Severe
All aged 15+	3.46	12.85	1.39	10.78	3.88	15.05	3.76	15.36
Women aged 15+	3.58	13.24	1.55	12.50	4.32	15.65	3.96	17.16
Men aged 15+	3.34	12.44	1.22	8.98	3.36	14.33	3.54	13.45
All aged 15-39	1.36	5.84	0.60	5.26	1.01	6.10	1.49	7.39
Women aged 15–39	1.25	6.2	0.54	5.86	0.99	6.42	1.31	7.63
Men aged 15-39	1.47	5.45	0.67	4.63	1.02	5.68	1.68	7.13
All aged 40-49	3.02	16	0.92	11.60	3.20	16.55	2.60	18.55
Women aged 40-49	3.77	15.58	1.21	15.31	3.85	17.57	2.57	21.90
Men aged 40-49	2.3	16.4	0.66	8.15	2.46	15.36	2.64	15.16
All aged 50-64	6.82	28.89	2.59	22.58	5.61	26.76	8.73	36.20
Women aged 50-64	9.11	33.71	3.29	26.54	5.81	27.67	8.03	39.89
Men aged 50-64	4.41	23.85	1.85	18.37	5.39	25.82	9.60	31.60
All aged 65+	19.44	48.68	8.75	46.93	20.69	55.09	23.24	62.70
Women aged 65+	20.81	53.26	8.94	50.21	24.14	55.09	27.24	67.59
Men aged 65+	18.53	45.61	7.40	42.88	16.36	48.75	18.36	56.71

Sources Author's calculations using Ethiopia Rural Socioeconomic Survey (2011/12), Malawi Integrated Household Survey (2010/11), Tanzania National Panel Survey (2010/11), Uganda National Panel Survey (2009/10)

Notes Each number is the share of the population in a given age group who reports experiencing a certain level of difficulty for one of the six domains of the Washington Group short set of questions. A severe difficulty includes reporting "a lot of difficulty" or "being unable to do" for at least one domain.

Moderate and Severe difficulty includes reporting at least "some difficulty" in at least one domain. Estimates are weighted.

follows: 3.46% in Ethiopia, 1.39% in Malawi, 3.88% in Tanzania, and 3.76% in Uganda. While Malawi seems to be somewhat of an outlier with lower prevalence rates, the other countries have rates that are relatively close to each other.

Overall, these prevalence estimates are consistent with the results of recent studies using the Washington Group questions in LMICs: for severe difficulties, 9.6% in Maldives (age 5+) (Loeb 2016), 8.5% in Zambia (all ages) (Eide and Loeb 2006), and 3.3% in South Africa (5 years and older) (Statistics South Africa 2015). For moderate and severe difficulties, 13.6% in Uganda (all ages) (UBOS 2016) and 9.1% in Bangladesh (as reported in Loeb 2016). In the 2008 Tanzania Disability Survey with a threshold of at least one severe difficulty or two moderate difficulties, prevalence stands at 7.8% (NBS 2008) for persons age seven and older, which is in between the prevalence rates found in this study for severe disability (3.88%) and severe/moderate difficulties (15.05%). The prevalence of severe difficulties found in this study for four LICs are lower than those found in two HICs that have used the Washington Group questions: Israel (14.8% for persons 20 years or older) and in the USA (9.5% for persons 18 years or older) (Loeb 2016).

4.3.1 Age

As expected, the prevalence of difficulties, whatever the severity, is higher for older age groups. For instance, in Ethiopia, 1.36% of adults age 15–39 have severe difficulties compared to 19.44% among people age 65 and older. This is further illustrated in Fig. 4.1 where the mean functional difficulty score is plotted by age for each country.[5] In all four countries, functional difficulties tend to increase with age among adults, especially from mid to late 40s. This result is consistent with much evidence worldwide that functional difficulties become more common with age (WHO–World Bank 2011; Mitra and Sambamoorthi 2014). There is also country evidence showing that prevalence increases with age in the four countries under study for functional difficulties (Wandera et al. (2014) and for other disability measures (CSA 2007; Payne et al. 2013). This finding contributes to fill the considerable gap on the functional status of older adults in LICs (Chatterji et al. 2015).

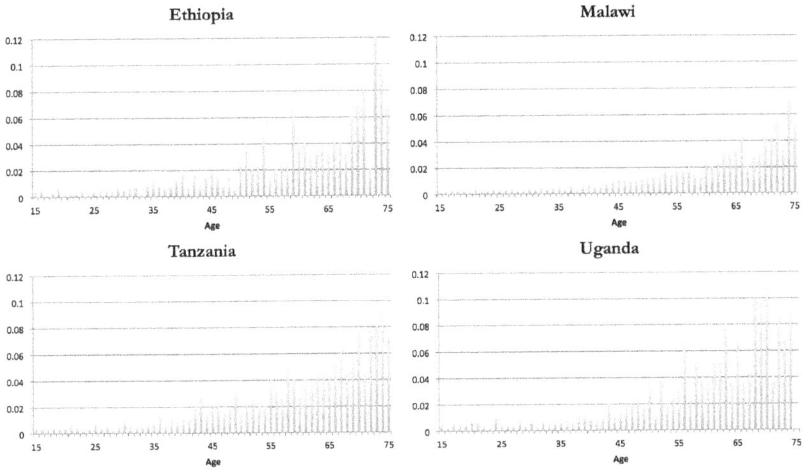

Fig. 4.1 Mean functional score by age. *Note* The upper limit of age is at 75 due to small sample sizes beyond that age

4.3.2 Sex

In Table 4.1, prevalence for all adults is higher among women than men in the four countries. The gender gap in prevalence is the largest in Malawi where the prevalence of moderate/severe difficulties is 3.5 percentage points higher among women (12.5 for women vs. 8.98 for men). The gender gap is not consistently found in all age groups for all countries. In fact, it is among adults age 50 and older that there is a gender gap in all countries. It is as large as 10 percentage points for moderate/severe difficulties in Ethiopia (aged 50–64) and Uganda (aged 65+). Based on the results for all four countries, women overall, but especially in older age groups are found to have higher prevalence than men. This result is consistent with findings on gender differences in disability from recent international studies among adults (e.g. Mitra and Sambamoorthi 2014; OECD 2003; WHO–World Bank 2011) and among older adults in high-income countries (Crimmings et al. 2011), while results of country level surveys and censuses are more mixed. For instance, for Uganda, the 2014 Census has a higher prevalence for women compared to men (14.5% vs 10%, respectively),[6] while for Tanzania, the 2008 Disability Survey found a rate of 7.8% for both men and women (NBS 2008).

More research is needed on the extent of a gender gap in prevalence, on gender differences in the determinants as well as the consequences of functional difficulties. Several gender-related factors may be at play in the higher prevalence among women including maternal care, access to healthcare, domestic violence, HIV/AIDS, and intra-household distribution of resources.

4.3.3 *Type of Functional Difficulty*

Figure 4.2 provides the distribution of difficulties by type of functional difficulty among persons with severe difficulties. Seeing and walking difficulties are the most common types of difficulties among persons with severe difficulties in all four countries. Hearing and cognitive difficulties are the third or fourth most common types of difficulties in the four countries. Communication difficulties are the least prevalent difficulties. A similar breakdown can be found within persons with moderate difficulties in Appendix A1 and persons with moderate and severe difficulties in Appendix A2. Comparing Fig. 4.2 and Appendix A1, seeing difficulties are more common among persons with moderate difficulties than severe difficulties.

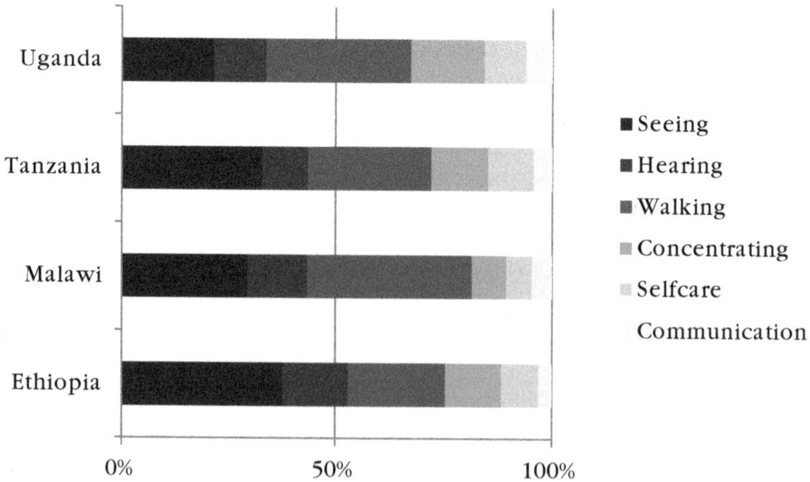

Fig. 4.2 Types of functional difficulties among persons with severe difficulties

These results above on difficulty types are consistent with results from several other studies in the four countries, although such studies do not all use the Washington Group short set of questions (e.g., Groce et al. 2014; Loeb and Eide 2004; NBS 2008; Wandera et al. 2014).

4.3.4 *Age at Onset*

In Tanzania and Uganda, respondents were asked about their age at the onset of the difficulty. Age at onset is important as it could be a determinant of wellbeing. An onset during childhood may impact education due to barriers to schools, which would affect school outcomes and in turn economic wellbeing later in life. An age of onset in the 50s would not impact individual educational outcomes but could still affect economic wellbeing, for instance, if the person does not retain her job. Figure 4.3 shows the distribution of age at onset in three age groups: birth to age 14, age 15–49, and age 50 and over. In both countries, about half of onsets took place at age 50 or over. Only 16% and 25% of persons with severe difficulties had an onset during childhood in Tanzania and Uganda, respectively. Information on age at onset is rarely available in surveys so far, so there is little to compare these results to. For Tanzania, this is overall consistent with results from the 2008 Disability Survey (NBS 2008) showing that functional difficulties arise at various ages.

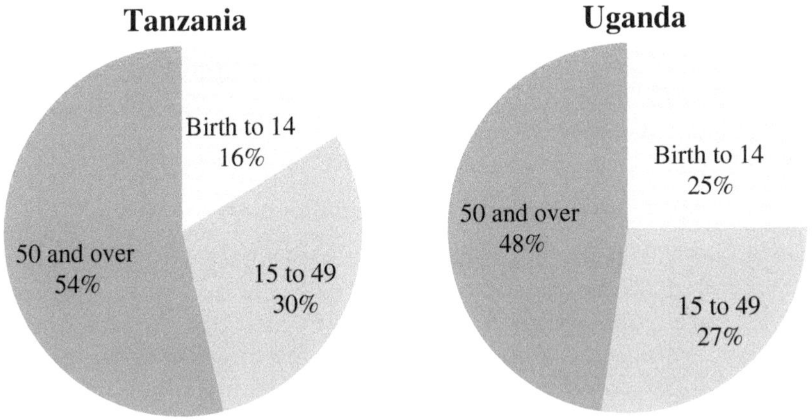

Fig. 4.3 Age of onset among persons with severe difficulties

Table 4.2 Prevalence of functional difficulties by mother's educational attainment

	Ethiopia	*Malawi*	*Tanzania*
Prevalence of severe difficulty			
Mother had no schooling	3.38%***	1.61%***	5.56%**
Mother had some schooling	0.89%	0.74%	1.39%
Prevalence of moderate and severe difficulty			
Mother had no schooling	12.03%***	12.44%***	20.77%**
Mother had some schooling	3.90%	9.60%	8.73%
Functional limitation score			
Mother had no schooling	0.01***	0.01***	0.03**
	(0.00)	(0.00)	(0.00)
Mother had some schooling	0.00	0.01	0.03
	(0.00)	(0.00)	(0.00)

Sources Author's calculations based on data described in the text and in Table 4.1 except for Ethiopia based on Ethiopia Rural Socioeconomic Survey 2013/2014. *Notes* For Uganda (both waves) and Ethiopia (wave 1), data on mother's education was largely missing. No result can be presented for Uganda. Estimates are weighted. ***indicates significance at 1% level of the difference compared to persons whose mother had some schooling. Statistical significance is tested with Pearson's Chi square test for prevalence and t-test for the functional score. For Tanzania, the category with 'no school' in fact refers to individuals with mothers with less than primary education. Standard errors are in parentheses.

4.3.5 *Mother's Educational Attainment*

Table 4.2 shows that the prevalence of functional difficulties and the functional score are significantly higher for persons whose mother had no schooling. For instance, in Ethiopia, 3.38% of persons whose mother had no schooling have a severe functional difficulty compared to only 0.89% for other individuals. This result has been found in at least one other study (Mont et al. 2014).

4.3.6 *Healthcare or Rehabilitation Measures Taken*

In Malawi, Tanzania, and Uganda, persons who reported at least one functional difficulty were asked if they took any measure to improve performance such as using assistive devices (e.g., glasses, braces, hearing aid), medication, surgical operation, spiritual/traditional means. Figure 4.4 shows the answers of respondents with at least one severe difficulty. More than 50% of people with severe difficulties do not take any measure to curb their difficulties. While more than a quarter of

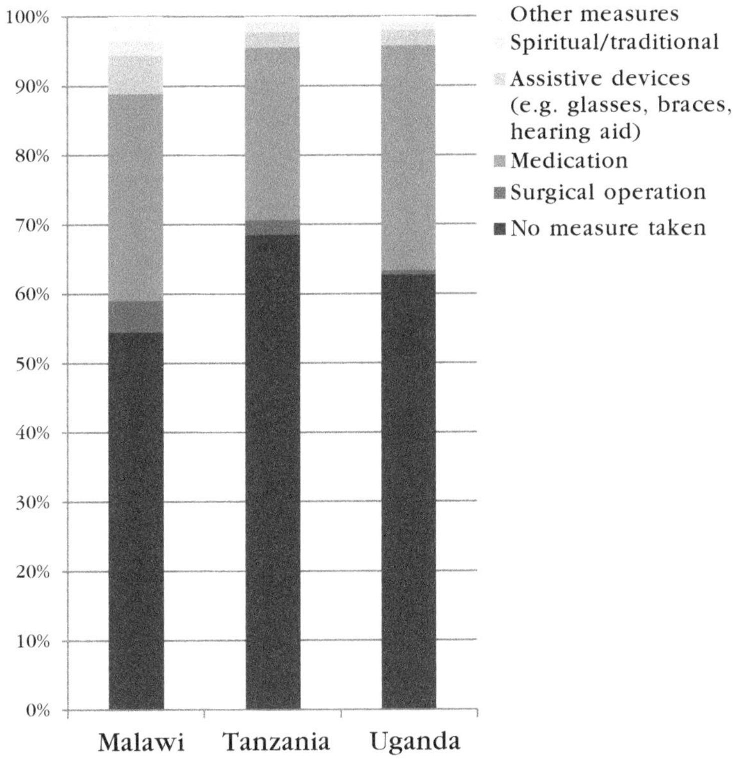

Fig. 4.4 Measure taken to improve performance at activities among persons with severe difficulties

individuals have used medication, a very small share has used assistive devices (e.g., glasses, wheelchairs). This could be due to a variety of reasons including the lack of availability of assistive devices or services, or their lack of affordability.

More broadly, results in Fig. 4.4 suggest that rehabilitation needs are large in Africa and are rarely fulfilled in a healthcare setting (Mulumba et al. 2014). No significant gender difference is found in the extent to which individuals took any measure to curb functional difficulties,[7] which is different from results in May-Teerink (1999) for Uganda.

This result is consistent with earlier research in Africa and in low-income settings in general.[8] The potential to prevent functional difficulties such as seeing and hearing has been noted globally, in LMICs and in Africa in particular.[9] This result points toward the need for secondary prevention in the form of assistive technology, rehabilitation services in low-income settings that can help curb functional difficulties. The prevention of functional difficulties through assistive technology, rehabilitation or healthcare needs to receive more attention and resources in human development whether from individual countries or international stakeholders.

The results above are also consistent with a small literature on disparities in access to care across disability status in LMICs. WHO–World Bank (2011) shows that persons with disabilities face barriers in accessing care. World Bank (2009) and Trani et al. (2011) show that individuals with disabilities have a reduced access to healthcare in India and urban Sierra Leone, respectively.

4.3.7 Transitions Over Time

Disability is often characterized or assumed to be a static phenomenon but do functional difficulties change over time? This could have implications for the identification of the group of persons with disabilities and for policies aimed at improving wellbeing for this group. Table 4.3 gives additional prevalence estimates for Ethiopia and Uganda, where

Table 4.3 Prevalence of functional difficulties by severity and trajectory (%)

	Ethiopia		*Uganda*	
	Severe	*Moderate & severe*	*Severe*	*Moderate & severe*
Any wave	5.54	21.16	6.07	19.53
Wave 1	3.39	13.34	4.15	12.84
Wave 2	3.17	11.50	3.74	11.2
Both waves	1.17	5.58	1.82	4.51
Wave 2 only (increase in difficulty)	2.07	6.82	1.92	6.69
Wave 1 only (reduction in difficulty)	2.30	8.76	2.34	8.32

Source Author's calculations using a balanced panel from Ethiopia Rural Socioeconomic Survey (2011/2012, 2013/2014) and Uganda NPS (2009/2010, 2010/2011). *Notes* The sample sizes are 7913 for Ethiopia and 5990 for Uganda respectively. These are longitudinal stamples. Other notes from Table 4.1 apply. Estimates are weighted

functional difficulty questions were asked in two waves. Prevalence estimates are close in both waves: for instance, for severe functional difficulties in Uganda, they stand at 4.15 for wave 1 (2009/2010) and 3.74 in wave 2 (2010). However, these prevalence rates for both waves capture in part different people. Indeed, only 1.82% of individuals report a severe difficulty in both waves in Uganda. There is thus some transitioning in and out of severe difficulties. These transitions may be due to actual changes in the severity of functional difficulties over time or to changes in reporting behavior. Perhaps some individuals may get used to experiencing functional difficulties, especially in the context of aging, and may stop reporting them. Changes between waves could also reflect some measurement error, as noted by Altman (2001).

This churning is consistent with transitions in disability status found in the literature in the context of HICs (Burchardt 2000; Burchardt 2003; Burkauser and Daly 1996; Drum 2014; Gannon and Nolan 2007; Jenkins and Rigg 2003) and in relation to aging (Grundy and Glaser 2000; Maddox et al. 1994). This literature has shown that transitions into or out of disability status are not rare. A small but growing literature on disability transitions can also be found in middle-income countries such as China (e.g., Liang et al. 2001) and Mexico (Diaz-Venegas et al. 2016a, b). In Malawi, Payne et al. (2013) find a relatively high number of transitions between disability states (none, moderate, severe) using an SF12 measure of functional status.[10]

4.3.8 Descriptive Statistics

Table 4.4 shows descriptive characteristics for individuals across functional status. First, it shows the share of respondents who answered for themselves instead of via a proxy. In Ethiopia, all individuals responded for themselves while in other countries, the share varies between about half to 90%. In Malawi, Tanzania, and Uganda, persons with functional difficulties are more likely to have responded to questions themselves perhaps suggesting different reporting behavior for functional difficulties between self reports and proxy reports.

Table 4.4 indicates that moderate and severe functional difficulties are associated with a somewhat different profile. In terms of personal factors, persons with functional difficulties are significantly older and more often female. With respect to resources, persons with functional difficulties are more likely to have a mother with no schooling in Ethiopia and Malawi

Table 4.4 Descriptive Statistics of sample of individuals

	Ethiopia			*Malawi*			*Tanzania*			*Uganda*		
	Severe	Moderate	None	Severe	Moderate	None	Severe	Moderate	None	Severe	Moderate	None
Self respondent	1.00	1.00	1.00	0.60	0.69	0.47	0.78***	0.91***	0.84	0.58***	0.73***	0.46
<u>Personal factors:</u>												
Age 15-39	0.27***	0.32***	0.73	0.31***	0.35***	0.75	0.16***	0.27***	0.67	0.28***	0.36***	0.76
Age 40-49	0.12***	0.20***	0.14	0.08***	0.14***	0.12	0.13***	0.20***	0.16	0.09***	0.18***	0.12
Age 50-64	0.22***	0.27***	0.09	0.19***	0.22***	0.09	0.20***	0.26***	0.12	0.25***	0.26***	0.08
Age 65+	0.39***	0.21***	0.04	0.42***	0.29***	0.04	0.51***	0.28***	0.05	0.38***	0.21***	0.03
Male	0.48	0.48*	0.50	0.43*	0.40***	0.50	0.39**	0.45*	0.46	0.46	0.42***	0.50
<u>Resources:</u>												
Mother no schooling [1]	0.98**	0.99***	0.93	0.97***	0.94***	0.94	0.86***	0.81***	0.63	NA	NA	NA
<u>Structural factors:</u>												
Household:												
Married	0.58***	0.71***	0.63	0.50***	0.61	0.62	0.36***	0.53**	0.47	0.38***	0.54***	0.49
Head	0.60***	0.53***	0.35	0.56***	0.57***	0.40	0.53***	0.59***	0.40	0.51***	0.57***	0.31
hh size	4.25***	5.42***	5.88	3.43***	3.37***	3.87	3.45	3.39***	3.53	7.81***	7.78***	8.46
	(0.16)	(0.11)	(0.34)	(0.13)	(0.05)	(0.02)	(0.12)	(0.06)	(0.03)	(0.45)	(0.22)	(0.08)

(continued)

Table 4.4 (continued)

	Ethiopia			*Malawi*			*Tanzania*			*Uganda*		
	Severe	Moderate	None	Severe	Moderate	None	Severe	Moderate	None	Severe	Moderate	None
Community:												
Distance to healthcare services	15.85 (1.12)	14.74 (0.60)	15.34 (0.23)	29.21 (13.58)	23.73 (4.63)	22.33 (13.58)	6.11 (0.79)	5.10 (0.33)	5.79 (0.79)	30.14*** (2.97)	26.12 (1.30)	24.85 (0.58)
Rural	NA	NA	NA	0.93***	0.87***	0.83	0.78***	0.71	0.69	0.87***	0.83***	0.76
N	*345*	*897*	*8,323*	*406*	*2,698*	*26,056*	*349*	*1,028*	*8,275*	*330*	*936*	*5,318*

Notes Notes of Table 4.1 apply. hh stands for household. Table includes sample means and standard errors (between brackets). ***, **, * indicate significance at 1%, 5% and 10% levels respectively of the difference compared to persons with no difficulty. Statistical significance is tested with t-test for continuous variable, Pearson's Chi square test for binary variables and the Wilcoxon-Mann-Whitney test for ordinal variables (age group). Distance to healthcare services refers to the distance to the nearest facility in kilometers (health clinic or post or hospital)

1. For Tanzania, this shows the share of individuals with mothers with less than primary education

and with less than primary schooling in Tanzania.[11] Regarding structural factors, persons with functional difficulties tend to live in smaller households are more often household heads and less often married. No consistent difference is found with respect to healthcare services. Persons with severe functional difficulties on average live further away from a health clinic but the difference is statistically significant only in Uganda.

4.4 Prevalence at the Household Level

Prevalence estimates at the household level are shown in Table 4.5. When the focus is on severe difficulties, prevalence estimates stand at 8.06% in rural Ethiopia, 3.35% in Malawi, 8.85% in Tanzania, and 10.01% in Uganda. Like at the individual level, Malawi is an outlier with

Table 4.5 Prevalence of functional difficulties among households (%)

	Ethiopia	*Malawi*	*Tanzania*	*Uganda*
Severe difficulty				
Overall				
– current wave	NA	3.35	8.85	10.01
– current or later wave	NA	NA	NA	14.41
Rural				
– current wave	8.06	3.68	5.64	11.05
– current or later wave	12.60	NA	NA	15.28
Urban				
– current wave	NA	1.5	10.74	5.72
– current or later wave	NA	NA	NA	10.85
Moderate and severe difficulty				
Overall				
– current wave	NA	21.96	29.80	37.18
– current or later wave	NA	NA	NA	44.76
Rural				
– current wave	26.42	22.64	25.60	36.87
– current or later wave	38.51	NA	NA	47.42
Urban				
– current wave	NA	18.07	32.35	24.38
– current or later wave	NA	NA	NA	33.83

Notes NA indicates not available. For each country the current wave refers to the one listed in Table 4.1. For Ethiopia, the later wave is Ethiopia Rural Socioeconomic Survey (2013/2014). For Uganda, the later wave is Uganda National Panel Survey (2010/2011). For Ethiopia, the current wave covers rural areas only, while the later wave also covers small towns. Hence, estimates for urban areas are not available for Ethiopia. Estimates are weighted

a lower household prevalence estimate compared to the other three countries where one in 10–12 households has at least one severe functional difficulty. Functional difficulties of any degree affect between one in five households in Malawi (21.80%) to more than one in three households in Uganda (34.4%). Functional difficulties of any degree thus seem relatively common among households. There is no consistent pattern across rural and urban areas. Prevalence is higher in rural areas in Malawi and Uganda but the opposite is true in Tanzania.

For Ethiopia and Uganda, where longitudinal data on functional difficulties is available, Table 4.5 also presents prevalence estimates for functional difficulties in any wave, leading as expected to higher rates: for instance, 12.60% and 14.41% of households have an adult with a severe difficulty in at least one wave in rural Ethiopia and in Uganda, respectively, with thus an increase in the prevalence rates of 4 percentage points.

Table 4.6 provides prevalence rates by household economic status. The Malawi, Tanzania, and Uganda datasets have information on

Table 4.6 Prevalence of functional difficulties among households and economic inequalities (%)

	Malawi	*Tanzania*	*Uganda*
Severe difficulty			
Below $1.90 poverty line			
– current wave	4.06***	15.80***	12.03**
– current wave or later wave	NA	NA	15.98
At or above $1.90 poverty line			
– current wave	2.58	8.64	8.1
– current wave or later wave	NA	NA	12.94
Moderate and severe difficulty			
Below $1.90 poverty line			
– current wave	22.26	36.59***	36.3
– current wave or later wave	NA	NA	46.67
At or above $1.90 poverty line			
– current wave	21.54	30.9	32.65
– current wave or later wave	NA	NA	42.96

Notes No result is available for Ethiopia due to a lack of data on consumption expenditures. For each country the current wave refers to the one listed in Table 1 (Notes). For Uganda, the later wave is Uganda National Panel Survey (2010/2011). Estimates are weighted. Per capita expenditures is total household expenditures divided by adult equivalent. ***, **indicate significance at 1% and 5% levels respectively of the difference in prevalence between households below the $1.90 poverty line compared to households at or above the $1.90 poverty line. Statistical significance is tested with Pearson's Chi square test

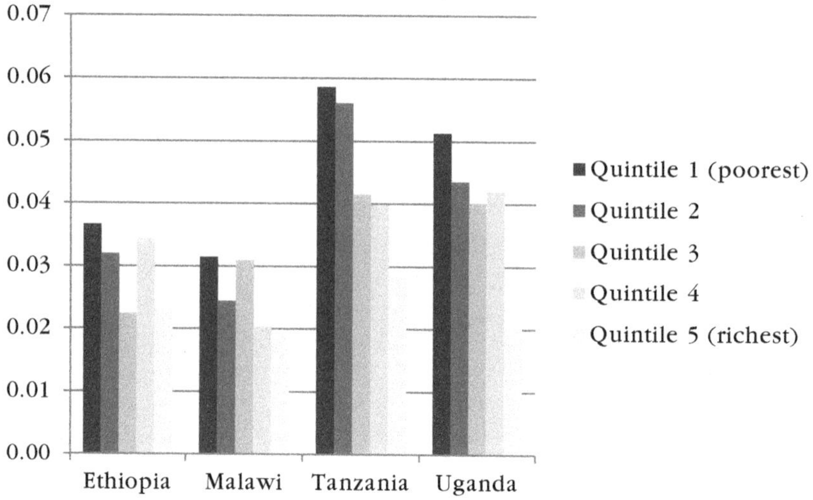

Fig. 4.5 Mean household functional score by asset index quintile

household consumption expenditures, which makes it possible to calculate the poverty headcount using the international poverty line of $1.90. Severe functional difficulties are more common for households below the poverty line. For instance, in Uganda, 12.03% of households below the $1.90 poverty line have an adult with a severe functional difficulty, compared to 8.1% for households beyond the poverty line. The share of households in poverty with an adult with a severe difficulty goes up to almost 15.98% in Uganda if one includes reports of functional difficulties in the current or following wave.

By quintile, whether by asset index or per capita consumption expenditure, there is not always a linear gradient of prevalence rates, but prevalence is consistently higher in the bottom quintile compared to the top one. This is shown in Fig. 4.5 where the mean household functional score of each quintile of asset index is plotted for each quintile in each country.

Comparing the poorest and richest quintiles, there is a consistent contrast between the poorest and the richest quintiles in Fig. 4.5.

This is consistent with results in Fig. 4.6, which shows the prevalence of severe functional difficulties in the poorest and richest quintiles. The difference is striking in the four countries with a prevalence two to four

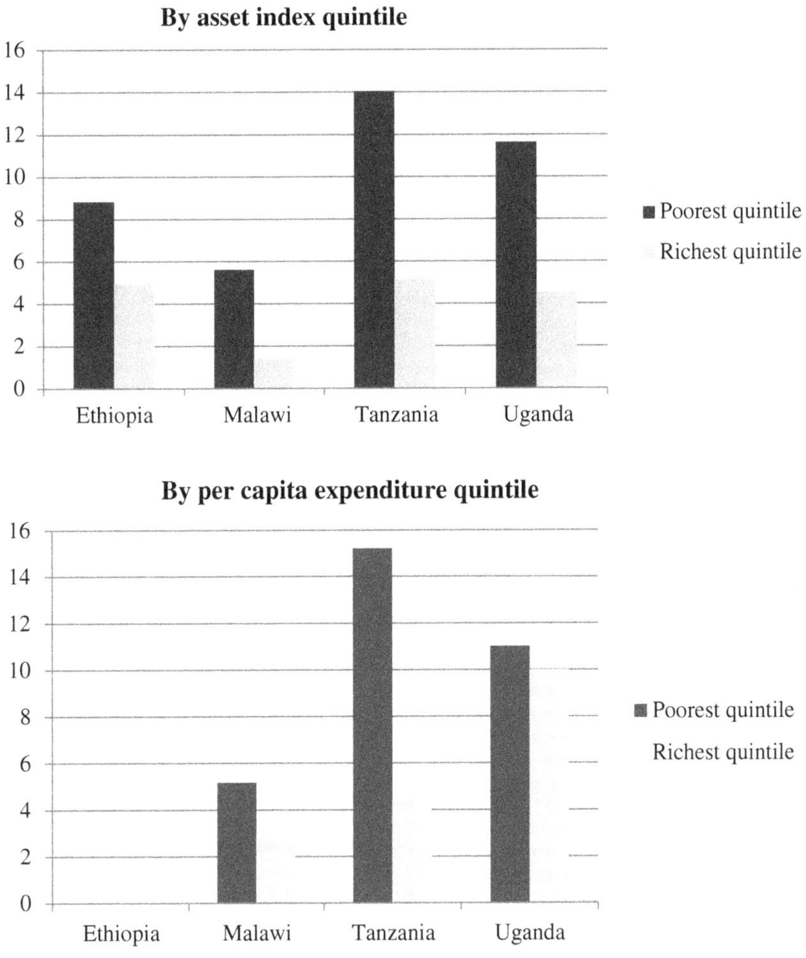

Fig. 4.6 Prevalence of severe functional difficulties for the poorest and richest quintiles (%)

times higher in the bottom quintile compared to the top quintile. For instance, in Tanzania, 14% of households in the bottom asset index quintile have a severe functional limitation, compared to 5% in the top quintile. As noted by Grech (2015), there is a common guess-estimate that one in five of the poorest people have a disability. Defining the poorest as those in the bottom quintile, prevalence estimates in Fig. 4.6 are below this guess-estimate for severe functional difficulties but above in Appendix A3 for moderate or severe difficulties. For Tanzania, for example, one in seven of the poorest have a severe functional difficulty and one in three have a severe or moderate difficulty. Other countries' estimates are close to the Tanzania estimates (Fig. 4.6 and Appendix A3).[12]

This result is consistent with results from Hosseinpoor et al. (2013) using an asset quintile, a disability measure similar to that in WHO–World Bank (2011) and 2002–2004 World Health Survey data for 49 countries, including Ethiopia and Malawi.

Table 4.7 gives descriptive statistics of households across functional status. It shows that households with functional difficulties have different characteristics in terms of structural factors. Households with functional difficulties have heads who tend to be older and less often female or married. They are significantly smaller households and tend to have more older or female members. They are also more likely to be in rural areas. For these characteristics, significant differences are found between households with severe or moderate functional difficulties, on the one hand, and households with no difficulty, on the other. However, the differences are larger for households with severe vs. moderate functional difficulties.

4.5 Conclusion: Summary and Implications

This chapter has several noteworthy results on disability prevalence for Ethiopia, Malawi, Tanzania, and Uganda.

1. The prevalence of moderate and severe functional difficulties among adults ranges from 10.8 to 15.1%, while the prevalence of severe difficulties alone spans 1.4–3.9%.
2. In the four countries, prevalence of functional difficulties at the household level ranges from one in five to one in three households.

Overall, this chapter shows that functional difficulties affect sizeable shares of individuals and households in Ethiopia, Malawi, Tanzania, and Uganda and thus require policy and research attention.

3. Persons with functional difficulties are a diverse group in terms of demographics (age, sex) but also with respect to age at onset, type of functional difficulty, and severity.

Table 4.7 Household descriptive statistics

	Ethiopia			*Malawi*			*Tanzania*			*Uganda*		
	Severe	Moderate	None	Severe	Moderate	None	Severe	Moderate	None	Severe	Moderate	None
Structural factors:												
Household :												
Age of head	57.39***	51.48***	43.37	58.06***	52.89***	39.39	60.11***	53.32***	42.32	60.67***	51.01***	40.13
	(1.48)	(0.76)	(0.36)	(1.31)	(0.48)	(0.19)	(1.27)	(0.79)	(0.44)	(1.13)	(0.77)	(0.78)
Head is married	0.68***	0.77***	0.83	0.58***	0.64***	0.75	0.45	0.54***	0.49	0.54***	0.63***	0.78
Head is male	0.71***	0.77***	0.82	0.63***	0.68***	0.78	0.51**	0.72***	0.76	0.62	0.63	0.77
Head has no formal education	0.24***	0.34***	0.44	0.44***	0.27***	0.22	0.41***	0.28**	0.20	0.75***	0.62***	0.73
hh size	4.34***	5.38	5.24	4.31	4.25**	4.47	3.37***	3.22***	2.74	7.00***	6.42***	5.78
	(0.18)	(0.12)	(0.05)	(0.16)	(0.06)	(0.03)	(0.15)	(0.08)	(0.05)	(0.51)	(0.19)	(0.09)
Share of hh members under age 15	0.30***	0.40***	0.44	0.27***	0.32***	0.40	0.23*	0.25***	0.30	0.35***	0.37***	0.43
	(0.02)	(0.01)	(0.01)	(0.02)	(0.01)	(0.00)	(0.02)	(0.01)	(0.01)	(0.02)	(0.01)	(0.01)
Share of hh members over age 60	0.24***	0.13***	0.07	0.28***	0.22***	0.06	0.29***	0.18***	0.06	0.25***	0.15***	0.06
	(0.02)	(0.01)	(0.00)	(0.02)	(0.10)	(0.00)	(0.03)	(0.02)	(0.01)	(0.02)	(0.01)	(0.00)

(continued)

Table 4.7 (continued)

	Ethiopia			*Malawi*			*Tanzania*			*Uganda*		
	Severe	Moderate	None	Severe	Moderate	None	Severe	Moderate	None	Severe	Moderate	None
Share of male hh members	0.47*** (0.02)	0.49*** (0.01)	0.50 (0.01)	0.43*** (0.02)	0.45*** (0.01)	0.50 (0.00)	0.45*** (0.02)	0.48*** (0.01)	0.51 (0.01)	0.50*** (0.02)	0.48* (0.01)	0.50 (0.01)
Community:												
Distance to healthcare services	15.64 (1.16)	15.40 (0.73)	15.86 (0.44)	20.71 (10.64)	26.95 (5.97)	21.30 (2.53)	6.08 (0.66)	4.54 (0.35)	5.54 (0.32)	29.90 (3.52)	27.95 (1.73)	25.48 (1.17)
Rural area	0.99	0.99	1.00	0.94	0.87***	0.84	0.77***	0.68***	0.65	0.882**	0.85***	0.77
N	*295*	*657*	*2,710*	*359*	*2,011*	*8,591*	*226*	*549*	*1,701*	*275*	*639*	*1,557*

Notes Table includes sample means and standard errors (between brackets). hh stands for household. ***, **, * indicate significance at 1%, 5% and 10% levels respectively of the difference compared to persons with no difficulty. Statistical significance is tested with t-test for continuous variable and Pearson's Chi square test for binary variables. Distance to healthcare services refers to the distance to the nearest facility in kilometers (health clinic or post or hospital)

4. There are also some patterns. They tend to affect older individuals more, as well as women more often than men. Seeing and walking limitations are the most prevalent limitations in the four countries. A majority of individuals do not take any measure to reduce their functional difficulties, suggesting there may be scope for prevention.
5. There is a strong socioeconomic gradient in prevalence. In fact, comparing the poorest and richest quintiles based on an asset index, prevalence is two to four times higher in the poorest quintile.

More research on gender is needed given the higher prevalence found among women in this study and in other studies. Functional difficulties are significantly associated with aging in the four countries. More research is also needed on older adults in less-resourced settings, for whom, little is known on health and wellbeing. These results overall suggest that functional status needs to be considered and included as part of aging, gender, public health, and broadly as part of human development policy and research.

The estimates in this book are of course not the final word on disability prevalence in Ethiopia, Malawi, Tanzania, and Uganda. They likely offer a lower bound estimate of prevalence given that only six functional difficulties are measured. More data collection efforts are needed to inform policy further. For instance, data using the extended set of questions of the Washington Group would offer information on mental health related functional difficulties (e.g., Loeb 2016). Surveys that can collect detailed information on the environment would provide information to help understand the determinants of functional difficulties. Because functional difficulties affect sizeable shares of individuals and households in the four countries under study, a study of the association and causal links between such difficulties and wellbeing inequalities is thus warranted and is conducted in the rest of this book.

Notes

1. Each answer is on a scale of 1–5: (1) no difficulty; (2) mild difficulty; (3) moderate difficulty; (4) severe difficulty; (5) extreme difficulty/unable to do. The disability score aggregates all answers, including mild and moderate and ranges from zero to 100. An Item Response Theory approach using a Rasch model was applied to construct the disability score. It is

compared to a threshold so as to identify who experiences a significant disability. This threshold was set at 40, which is the average of the disability scores of people who report at least one extreme limitation on any of the items and/or a chronic health condition (e.g., asthma, arthritis, diabetes, depression) explaining that 'such chronic diseases are associated with disability, it is justifiable to use them as indicator conditions for estimating the average levels of functioning across all the chronic conditions that were assessed in the WHS, in order to set a meaningful threshold.' (WHO–World Bank 2011).

2. Disability prevalence estimates that are not standardized are available in the working paper version of Mitra and Sambamoorthi (2014) available at: http://papers.ssrn.com/sol3/papers.cfm?abstract_id=2329676.
3. Ethiopia is not unique in the vast range of disability estimates it receives. Another example among the countries under study is Malawi: 3.8% using the 2008 Census (NSO 2010); 4.2% as per Loeb and Eide (2004); 14% in WHO–World Bank (2011).
4. It should be noted that prevalence estimates had very low standard errors producing very narrow confidence intervals, which are not presented.
5. The median is zero and is therefore not used.
6. A number of other studies in LMICs also find a higher prevalence among women compared to men (Mexico: Diaz-Venegas et al. 2016a; Bangladesh: Moniruzzaman et al. 2016).
7. Sex-disaggregated results are not reported here.
8. See for instance, Borg et al. (2011), Eide and Øderud (2009), May-Teerink (1999), Magnusson et al. (2013), Harniss et al. (2015), McPherson (2014), WHO (2011).
9. Global Burden of Disease collaborators Study 2016; Kulua et al. (2011), Muller et al. (2011), Lewallen and Courtright (2001).
10. SF12 is a twelve-item functional health measure. More information can be found in Burdine et al. (2000).
11. This information is not available in Uganda.
12. This result also holds using per capita expenditures, with for instance in Malawi 5.17% with severe functional limitations in the lowest quintile and 2.78% in the highest quintile (this result is not shown in Tables/graphs).

References

Altman, B. M. (2001). Definitions of disability and their operationalization. In Barnartt, S. N. & Altman, B. M. (eds) (2001). *Exploring theories and expanding methodologies: where we are and were we need to go*, pp. 77–100. Research in Social Science and Disability (Vol. 2). Amsterdam: JAI Elsevier science.

Borg, J., Lindström, A., & Larsson, S. (2011). Assistive technology in developing countries: A review from the perspective of the convention on the rights of persons with disabilities. *Prosthetics and Orthotics International, 35*(1), 20–29. doi:10.1177/0309364610389351.

Burchardt, T. (2000). The dynamics of being disabled. *Journal of Social Policy, 29*(4), 645–668.

Burchardt, T. (2003). *Being and becoming: Social exclusion and the onset of disability.* ESRC Centre for Analysis of Social Exclusion (CASE) report 21.

Burdine, J. N., Felix, M. R., Abel, A. L., Wiltraut, C. J., & Musselman, Y. J. (2000). The SF-12 as a population health measure: An exploratory examination of potential for application. *Health Services Research, 35*(4), 885–904.

Burkhauser, R. V., & Daly, M. C. (1996). Employment and economic well-being following the onset of a disability: The role for public policy. In J. Mashaw, V. Reno, R. V. Burkhauser, & M. Berkowitz (Eds.), *Disability, work, and cash benefits* (pp. 59–102). Kalamazoo, MI: W.E. Upjohn Institute for Employment Research.

Chatterji, S., Byles, J., Cutler, D., Seeman, T., & Verdes, E. (2015). Health, functioning, and disability in older adults-present status and future implications. *Lancet, 385,* 563–575.

Crimmings, E. M., Kim, J. K., & Solé-Auro, A. (2011). Gender differences in health: Results from SHARE, ELSA and HRS. *The European Journal of Public Health, 21*(1), 81–91.

CSA. (2007). *The 2007 population and housing census.* Addis Ababa: Central Statistical Agency of Ethiopia.

Diaz-Venegas, C., Reistetter, T. A., & Wong, R. (2016a). Differences in the progression of disability: A U.S.–Mexico comparison. *Journals of Gerontology: Social Sciences.* Accessed 19 July 2016.

Diaz-Venegas, C., Reistetter, T. A., Wang C. -Y., & Wong, R. (2016b). The Progression of disability among older adults in Mexico. *Disability & Health.* Accessed Jan 5 2016.

Drum, C. E. (2014). The dynamics of disability and health conditions. *Disability and Health, 7,* 2–5.

Eide, A. H., & Loeb, M. (2006). *Living conditions among people with activity limitations in Zambia. A representative national study.* SINTEF Report STF78 A262. Oslo: SINTEF.

Eide, A. H., & Øderud, T. (2009). Assistive devices in low-income countries. In MacLachlan & Swartz (Eds.), pp. 149–160.

Gannon, B., & Nolan, B. (2007). Transitions in disability and work. *Estudios de Economía Aplicada, 25*(2), 447–472.

Grech, S. (2015). *Disability and poverty in the global south. Renegotiating development in Guatemala.* London: Palgrave Macmillan.

Groce, N., Murray, B., & Kealy, A. (2014). *Disabled beggars in Addis Ababa: Current situation and prospects for change.* Geneva: International Labour Organization.

Gundy, E., & Glaser, K. (2000). Socio-demographic differences in the onset and progression of disability in early old age: A longitudinal study. *Age and Ageing, 29*(2), 149–157.

Harniss M., Samant Raja D., & Matter R. (2015). Assistive technology access and service delivery in resource-limited environments: Introduction to a special issue of disability and rehabilitation: Assistive technology. *Disability and Rehabilitation Assistive Technology, 10*(4), 267–270. doi:10.3109/17483107.2015.1039607. Epub 8 May 2015.

Hosseinpoor, A. R., Stewart Williams, J. A., Gautam, J., Posarac, A., Officer, A., Verdes, E., et al. (2013). Socioeconomic inequality in disability among adults: A multicountry study using the World Health Survey. *American Journal of Public Health, 103*(7), 1278–1286.

Jenkins, S. P., & Rigg, J. A. (2003). *Disability and disadvantage: Selection, onset, and duration effects.* (Institute for Social and Economic Research (ISER) Working Papers Number 2003–18).

Kalua, K., Lindfield, R., Mtupanyama, M., Mtumodzi, D., & Msiska V. (2011). Findings from a rapid assessment of avoidable blindness (RAAB) in Southern Malawi. *PLoS One, 6*(4), e19226.

Lewallen, S., & Courtright, P. (2001). Blindness in Africa. *British Journal of Ophtalmology, 85,* 897–903.

Liang, J., Liu, X., & Gu, S. (2001). Transitions in functional status among older people in Wuhan, China: Socioeconomic differentials. *Journal of Clinical Epidemiology, 54*(11), 1126–1138.

Loeb, M. (2016). International census/Survey data and the short set of disability questions developed by the Washington Group on disability statistics. In Altman (Ed.), pp. 255–304.

Loeb, M., & Eide, A. (2004). *Living conditions among people with activity limitations in Malawi.* Oslo: SINTEF Health Research.

Maddox G.L., Clark D.O., & Steinhauser K. (1994). Dynamics of functional impairment in late adulthood. *Social Science and Medicine, 38,* 925–936.

Magnusson, L., Ahlström, G., Ramstrand, N., & Fransson, E. I. (2013). Malawian prosthetic and orthotic users' mobility and satisfaction with their lower limb assistive device. *Journal of Rehabilitation Medicine, 45*(4), 385–391.

May-Teerink, T. (1999). A survey of rehabilitative services and people coping with physical disabilities in Uganda, East Africa. *International Journal of Rehabilitation Research, 22*(4), 311–316.

McPherson, B. (2014). Hearing assistive technologies in developing countries: Background, achievements and challenges. *Disability and Rehabilitation Assistive Technology, 9*(5), 360–364. doi:10.3109/17483107.2014.907365. Epub 7 Apr 2014.

Mitra, S., & Sambamoorthi, U. (2014). Disability prevalence among adults: Estimates for 54 countries and progress toward a global estimate. *Disability and Rehabilitation, 36*, 940–947.

Moniruzzaman, M., Zaman, M. M., Mashreky, S. R., & Fazlur Rahman, A. K. M. (2016). Prevalence of disability in Manikganj district of Bangladesh: Results from a large-scale cross-sectional survey. *British Medical Journal Open, 6*.

Mont, D. (2007). Measuring Health and Disability. *Lancet*. 2007; 369: 1548–1663, and Social Protection Paper 0706, World Bank.

Mont, D., Cappa C., Bahadur, C. N., Dorji C., Hingst, G., Khan, N. (2014). Poverty, maternal education and child disability: Evidence from Bhutan, *Disability and International Development*.

Müller, A., Zerom, M., Limburg, H., Ghebrat, Y., Meresie, G., Fessahazion, K., et al. (2011). Results of a rapid assessment of avoidable blindness (RAAB) in Eritrea. *Ophthalmic Epidemiology, 18*(3), 103–108.

Mulumba, M., Nantaba, J., Brolan, C. E., Ruano, A. L., Brooker, K., & Hammonds, R. (2014). Perceptions and experiences of access to public healthcare by people with disabilities and older people in Uganda. *International Journal of Equity in Health, 13*, 76.

Murray, C. J. L., & Lopez, A. D. (Eds.). (1996). *The global burden of disease: A comprehensive assessment of mortality and disability from diseases, injuries and risk factors in 1990 and projected to 2020* (1st ed.). Cambridge: Harvard University Press.

NBS. (2008). *Disability survey report*. Tanzania National Bureau of Statistics. http://www.nbs.go.tz/nbstz/index.php/english/statistics-by-subject/health-statistics/disability-statistics/681-disability-survey-2008. Accessed 27 Jan 2017.

NDSD. (2015). *Elements of the financial and economic costs of disability to households in South Africa: A pilot study*. Pretoria: National Department of Social Development, Republic of South Africa.

NSO. (2010). *Malawi population and housing census*. Main Report.

OECD. (2003). *Transforming disability into ability: Policies to promote work and income security for persons with disabilities*. Paris: Organisation for Economic Cooperation and Development.

Payne, C. F., Mkandawire, J., & Kohler, H.-P. (2013). Disability transitions and health expectancies among adults 45 years and older in Malawi: A cohort-based model. *PLoS Medicine, 10*(5), e1001435. doi:10.1371/journal.pmed.1001435.

Statistics South Africa. (2014). *Census 2011: Profile of persons with disabilities in South Africa*. Pretoria: Republic of South Africa.

Trani, J. F., Browne, J., Kett, M., Bah, O., Morlai, T., Bailey, N., et al. (2011a). Health and reproductive health of people with disabilities: A cross sectional study in Sierra Leone. *Social Science and Medicine, 73*(10), 1477–1489.

Trani, J. F., Bakhshi, P., Bellanca, N., Biggeri, M., & Marchetta, F. (2011b). Disabilities through the capability approach lens: Implications for public policies. *Alter, European Journal of Disability Research, 5*(3), 143–157.

UBOS. (2016). *The national population and housing census 2014—Main report.* Kampala: Uganda Bureau of Statistics.

Wandera, S. O., Ntozi, J., & Kwagala, B. (2014). Prevalence and correlates of disability among older Ugandans: Evidence from the Uganda National Household Survey. *Global Health Action, 7,* 25686.

WHO. (2008). *The global burden of disease: 2004 update.* Geneva: World Health Organization.

WHO–World Bank. (2011). *World report on disability.* Geneva: World Health Organization.

World Bank. (2009). *People with disabilities in India: From commitments to outcomes.* Washington, DC: World Bank.

CHAPTER 5

Functional Difficulties and Inequalities Through a Static Lens

Abstract This chapter is about the association between disability and inequalities. Results from both descriptive statistics and regressions indicate that functional difficulties have significant and large associations with both individual and household deprivations in Ethiopia, Malawi, Tanzania, and Uganda. This is found through an indicator-by-indicator analysis as well as through an assessment of multidimensional poverty. There are four wellbeing dimensions for which functional difficulties were systematically associated with deprivations in the four countries: education, morbidity, employment, and economic security. Some persons with functional difficulties do achieve levels of wellbeing comparable to persons with no difficulty. The association between functional difficulties and deprivations was found for both severe and moderate functional difficulties, although it was typically larger and more often significant for the former.

Keywords Disability · Poverty · Multidimensional poverty · Gender · Aging · Africa

JEL I1 · I3 · O15

S. Mitra, *Disability, Health and Human Development*,
Palgrave Studies in Disability and International Development,
DOI 10.1057/978-1-137-53638-9_5

This chapter investigates the association between functional difficulties on the one hand, and different deprivations, on the other. For Ethiopia, Malawi, Uganda, and Tanzania, it uses cross-sectional LSMS data and thus draws a static snapshot of this association. Framing this question within the human development model, the objective is to assess the association between functional difficulties and deprivations measured in terms of educational attainment, morbidity, employment, material wellbeing, economic security and through the experience of multidimensional poverty.

5.1 Literature on Inequalities Associated with Disability

Globally, the evidence on the wellbeing inequalities associated with disability is limited, although the situation greatly differs between HICs and LMICs. Most of the evidence pertains to HICs. Overall, in HICs, the evidence suggests that persons with disabilities have lower educational attainment and experience lower employment rates, lower wages when employed, and are more likely to be income poor (Brucker et al. 2015; Grammenos 2013). They are also more likely to be chronically poor (She and Livermore 2009). In LMICs, there is very limited empirical research on disability and poverty or deprivations in general (Groce et al. 2011; Grech 2015; Banks and Polack 2014). The peer-reviewed literature, while still small, has recently grown. The literature review below is limited to deprivations in dimensions of wellbeing later analyzed in this chapter and to peer reviewed papers published since 2000.[1] The qualitative evidence that gives space to the voices and perceptions of persons with disabilities is beyond the scope of this review.[2]

5.1.1 *Material Wellbeing*

This section starts with material wellbeing, typically measured through consumption expenditures, assets, and living conditions. There has not been consistent evidence of material deprivations for households with disabilities relative to other households. Hoogeveen (2005) (Uganda) and Mont and Cuong (2011) (Vietnam) find that households with disabilities have lower expenditures than households without, but Rischewski et al. (2008) (Rwanda) does not. A cross-country study of LMICs (Filmer 2008) finds that in eight out of 12 countries, disability in adulthood is associated with a higher probability of being in poverty, where poverty refers to belonging to the lowest two quintiles in terms of household expenditures or asset ownership. Another cross-country study (Mitra et al. 2013) finds a significant difference in household per capita expenditures across disability status in only three out of 15 LMICs.

There are, however, challenges in using household expenditures to assess the wellbeing of households with disabilities, as they may reflect additional expenditures associated with a disability (NDSD 2015). These expenditures may relate to general items that any household may need (e.g., healthcare, food) as well as to disability-specific items (e.g., assistive devices, rehabilitation), although this is perhaps less of a concern in the LICs under consideration in this study where disability-specific goods and services may not be available. Having similar or higher expenditures at the household level across disability status does not necessarily imply that the standard of living is similar. This empirical concern regarding the use of household expenditures is related to the conversion function and its particular relevance to disability, as discussed earlier in Chapter 2.

With respect to asset ownership, several studies show that households with disabilities have fewer assets and worse living conditions compared to other households.[3] However, Eide et al. (2003a) and Trani and Loeb (2010) find no significant difference in Zimbabwe and Afghanistan/Zambia, respectively. Mitra et al. (2013) find a significant difference in the rate of asset deprivation in only four of 15 LMICs.

5.1.2 *Educational Attainment*

There is extensive and consistent evidence that adults with disabilities have lower educational attainment in a number of LMICs.[4] This association consistently found among adults may result from lower school attendance among children with disabilities (Filmer 2008; Mizunoya et al. 2016), but may also be due to more frequent onsets among adults with limited educational attainment because they are more exposed to malnutrition, lack of access to healthcare, and risky working conditions.

5.1.3 *Employment*

How disability may impact employment is an empirical question, and realities in LMICs may differ from HICs. In an agrarian economy, as is often the case in LICs, many jobs are in the primary sector (agriculture, forestry, mining) and may involve heavy manual labor, which people with physical difficulties may not be able to do. People with hearing or cognition difficulties, on the other hand, may not experience barriers to physical labor. The effect of disability on employment will also depend on the workplace, its accessibility, available accommodations and transport, and whether there is discrimination that might prevent access to employment and/or might lead to lower wages (Baldwin and Johnson 2005; Mitra and Sambamoorthi 2008). The policy context is also relevant; for instance, vocational rehabilitation, disability insurance, or social assistance programs could facilitate, limit or not affect access to employment for persons with disabilities depending on how they are designed and implemented. In some LMICs (e.g., South Africa), social protection benefits have been introduced to provide financial support to persons with disabilities.

Several studies in LMICs find that persons with disabilities are less likely to be employed.[5] In a study of 15 countries, Mizunoya and Mitra (2013) have results that are somewhat mixed with a significant disability gap in employment rates in nine countries out of 15. In these nine countries with a disability gap, the size of the gap varies greatly across countries.

Finally, it should be noted that not working may not be an option. So people may be begging or selling small items on the roadside earning very little but working. Hence, the type of employment needs to be considered. In most LMICs, a large majority are in the informal sector. Some studies have shown that persons with disabilities are disproportionately more likely to be working in the informal sector than persons without disabilities (e.g., Adioetomo et al. 2014; Mizunoya and Mitra 2013).

5.1.4 Morbidity and Healthcare Expenditures

Disability is associated with a wide range of health conditions (WHO-World Bank 2011); some of which may result in morbidity and high healthcare needs. These may lead to higher health expenditures. Trani and Loeb (2010) also show that on average, 'persons with severe or very severe disabilities spent 1.3 times more on healthcare than non-disabled respondents' (p. 36). Mitra et al. (2013) show that households with disabilities have a higher ratio of medical to total expenditures in nine out of 15 countries while WHO-World Bank (2011) finds that persons with disabilities are more likely to experience catastrophic health expenditures.

Overall, in LMICs, there is not a consistent overall pattern of evidence on disability and deprivations. The evidence thus far points toward individuals with disabilities being worse off in terms of educational attainment, morbidity, and health expenditures, while in terms of employment and household material wellbeing, the evidence is more mixed.

5.1.5 Multidimensional Poverty

The literature review so far considered inequalities in one dimension of wellbeing at a time. Recently, several studies have found that disability is associated with a higher likelihood of experiencing multidimensional poverty (Mitra et al. 2013; Trani and Cunning 2013; Trani et al 2015, 2016). These deprivations can be in terms of employment, health, education, material wellbeing, social participation or psychological wellbeing. This growing literature has provided consistent evidence that in LMICs, disability is correlated with the experience of multidimensional poverty while the very nature of deprivations may vary across countries. For instance, it could be in terms of employment and healthcare access in one country, but in terms of educational attainment and living conditions in another.

This consistent association between disability and multidimensional poverty comes in contrast to the more mixed evidence on disability and material wellbeing. This literature, however, remains small and so far separate from the growing general research on multidimensional poverty. The MPI offers a measure of the experience of simultaneous deprivations at the household level and is increasingly used in policy and research (Alkire and Santos 2014). It is yet to present separate results for households with disabilities.

5.1.6 Overview

Deriving any definitive conclusion on inequalities across disability status is problematic in this literature with varying measures for disability, wellbeing indicators, data sources, and methodologies. First, studies use different methods: some studies only present means and frequency counts of economic indicators across disability status (e.g., Hoogeveen 2005), while other studies resort to multivariate analysis using a variety of empirical strategies which can be difficult to compare.[6] Some studies measure disability through functional difficulties (e.g., Mont and Cuong 2011), while others use broad activity limitations (e.g., Mitra 2008). Several of these studies (Mitra et al. 2013; Mizunoya and Mitra 2013; WHO-World Bank 2011) rely on the World Health Survey (WHS) that was designed to collect a detailed health and disability profile of individuals but provides only summary measures of economic wellbeing, for instance, on employment and household expenditures. Besides, not every individual in a household in the WHS was interviewed, only one individual per household. Hence, differences across disability status may be underestimated for household wellbeing indicators. Finally and more importantly, results vary across wellbeing dimensions, making the evidence mixed. It could be read in different ways. Someone relying on traditional poverty measures based on consumption expenditures or asset ownership data will not find any consistent significant association between disability and poverty. Someone relying on multidimensional poverty measures will. This is surprising given the consistent evidence found in HICs, whatever the measure of poverty.

As a result, despite a growing body of research on disability-related inequalities in LMICs, more work is needed with internationally comparable and tested disability measures and detailed economic indicators suitable to the LMIC context to understand disability and inequalities. Research is particularly needed in the context of LICs. Mizunoya and Mitra (2013) note that the six countries in this study that do not have a disability gap in employment are LICs, while only two of the nine countries with a disability gap (Bangladesh and Burkina Faso) are in the low-income category. This is consistent with the results on multidimensional poverty in Mitra et al. (2013). In both studies, the authors hypothesize that economic inequalities associated with disability may be more common in middle-income countries compared to LICs because as countries develop, there may be growing barriers to employment and economic activities for persons with disabilities. It could also be that disability is associated with premature mortality in LICs, more so than in middle-income countries, which would drive down the association between disability and economic deprivations. This chapter aims to fill some of these gaps in the literature by offering evidence for Ethiopia, Malawi, Tanzania, and Uganda.

5.2 Methodology

This Chapter presents for several indicators of wellbeing at the individual and household levels bivariate and multivariate analyses to investigate the association between functional difficulties and wellbeing in a number of domains. For this analysis, as described in Chapter 3, the following datasets are used: the 2010/11 Malawi Third Integrated Household Survey, the 2010/11 Tanzania National Panel Survey, the 2011/12 Ethiopia Rural Socioeconomic Survey and the 2009/10 Uganda National Panel Survey. The measures of moderate or severe functional difficulties and the functional score are as explained earlier in Chapter 3.

5.2.1 *Wellbeing Indicators*

The household and individual wellbeing indicators analyzed in this chapter are presented in Table 5.1. As explained in Chapter 3, they were chosen based on a review of the datasets and guidance from Stiglitz et al. (2009) for a list of dimensions of wellbeing. In the four countries, an index of assets and living conditions is used (Filmer and Pritchett 2001). Assets include ownership of a bike, a car, a refrigerator, a fixed-line telephone, a cell phone, a television set, and a computer. Living condition variables include building quality (high-quality floor and wall materials), water source (from pipes, from protected wells, and from unprotected sources), type of toilet (flush, latrine, other/none), and use of a gas or electric cooking stove.[7] The index is normalized to range from zero to 100 (Table 5.1).

For Malawi, Tanzania, and Uganda, a comprehensive range of annual expenditure variables are analyzed: total, total nonhealth, health,[8] and education.[9] In Ethiopia, expenditures were collected only on food items, so these expenditures-based indicators cannot be used. The monetary poverty status of the household is determined using the international $1.90 poverty line. Detailed income data from earned and unearned sources is not available in the four countries, but data on income received from social protection transfers is. Social Protection transfers include assistance received by the household from government or nongovernment institutions (such as church). Two measures of economic insecurity are also used. One covers food insecurity; it measures whether the household faced a situation where it did not have enough food. The other one measures if the household has experienced a shock recently.

Several issues should be noted with regard to using household (nonhealth) expenditures as a dimension of economic wellbeing in the context of this study. First, as pointed earlier, if poverty is measured

Table 5.1 Aspects of wellbeing and indicators

Wellbeing	*Indicators*
Household level:	
Assets/Living conditions	Asset index[1]
Household Consumption	Household's daily per capita expenditures (PCE) is under $1.90 a day
	Total expenditures: Annual expenditures for the household and in local currency
	Total expenditures (nonhealth): Annual expenditures for the household and in local currency
	Health expenditures: Annual expenditures for the household and in local currency
	Education expenditures: Annual expenditures for the household and in local currency
Income	Social protection transfers for the household in local currency per year[2]
Food insecurity	In the past 12 months, household respondent faced with a situation when did not have enough food to feed the household.
Shocks	Household experienced a shock recently[3]
Individual level:	
Educational attainment	Ever attended school
Morbidity	Sick or injured recently[4]
Work status	Worked in the past week[5]
	Hours worked[6]
	Type of work (family farm, family business, wage work, other work)

Notes [1]See text for details on the asset index

[2]Social protection transfers refer to assistance received by the household from government or nongovernment (such as church) institutions

[3]Each household was asked about shocks experienced in the past 12 months in Ethiopia, Malawi and Uganda and in the past 5 years in Tanzania. For each country, the question was asked for a list of under 20 types of shocks (e.g. drought or floods, livestock died or stoken, loss of land). A variable was constructed to indicate that a household experienced at least one shock

[4]For Malawi and Uganda, the question refers to an 'illness or injury' in the past 2 weeks and 30 days respectively. For Ethiopia, the question refers to 'a health problem' in the past 2 months. For Tanzania only, the question asks if the person visited a healthcare provider in the last 4 weeks: there is no question on recent health problem or illness/injury

[5]Work indicates if an individual worked in past 7 days or did not work in past 7 days but has a job to return to. Work can be of any type for pay, profit, barter or home use and also includes apprenticeships

[6]Hours worked refer to hours worked in the past week among individuals who worked in the past week. In all countries but Uganda, individuals were queried about hours worked by type of work (e.g. farm, business). In Uganda, work hours were asked for each day of the past week for the individual's main job and secondary job

through per capita expenditures (PCE) against a poverty line, the comparison of households with a functional difficulty to other households may be biased due to the conversion factors: households with disabilities may have additional (nonhealth) needs and hence expenditures (e.g., transportation, personal assistance) due to the functional difficulty. Evidence on the additional costs of living with a disability is available only in very few LMICs.[10] Second, there is the possibility that the intra-household distribution of expenditures is unequal across functional difficulty status. For these two reasons, PCE may not be an accurate indicator of economic disparities across functional difficulty status. In contrast, assets or living conditions, at least the ones included in this study as described earlier, can be, to a larger extent, considered as household common goods, so the issue of intra-household distribution is less likely to arise.

Several individual wellbeing indicators are also assessed. Educational attainment is used with an indicator of whether an individual ever attended school. Morbidity is captured by a question asking persons whether they recently experienced a health problem (illness or injury). However, for Tanzania, the question asks if the person visited a healthcare provider in the last 4 weeks; there is no question on recent health problem or illness/injury. Three labor market outcomes are analyzed: work status, hours worked during the last week, and work type. Work status refers to working in the past week or having a job to return to. Work types include working at a family-owned farm or business, a wage job (working for wage, salary or commission) or some other type of work (unpaid family worker or apprenticeship). For Ethiopia, Malawi, and Tanzania, individuals report hours of work during the past week in their first and second job or by type of job; these hours across jobs are added up to get weekly hours of work. For Uganda, daily hours of work are available for each day of the past week, which are added up.

Overall, and in the context of the human development model of Chapter 2, one kind of health deprivations (functional difficulties) is considered in its association with other deprivations related to education, morbidity, work, material wellbeing, and economic security.

5.2.2 *Multidimensional Poverty*

In addition to an indicator-by-indicator analysis, this study estimates a set of measures of multidimensional poverty developed by Alkire and Foster

(2011) to investigate the experience of simultaneous deprivations. This is in line with a multidimensional understanding of wellbeing and poverty in the capability approach in general, and in the human development model, in particular. In brief, this method counts deprivations for a set of dimensions that affect an individual at the same time. An individual is considered multidimensionally poor if the number of deprivations of the individual is equal or above a set threshold. Three multidimensional poverty measures are calculated. The poverty headcount H gives the percentage of the population who are multidimensionally poor. The average deprivation share A gives the share of deprivations experienced by the poor out of all of their dimensions. The adjusted headcount ratio M_0 is the product of H and A; in other words, it is the headcount ratio adjusted for the intensity of the deprivations experienced by the poor. It is on a continuum from 0 to 1. Details on the calculation of this set of measures are included in Box 2.

Box 2: The Alkire and Foster (2011) Multidimensional Poverty Measures

Dimensions are weighted: w_j is the weight of dimension j. Each individual i has a weighted count of dimensions where that person is deprived (c_i) across all measured dimensions: $0 \leq c_i \leq d$ where d is the number of dimensions; $c_i = \sum_{j=1}^{d} w_j c_{ij}$ with c_{ij} a binary variable equal to one if individual i is deprived in dimension j, and zero otherwise. Let q_i be a binary variable equal to one if the person is identified as poor, and to zero otherwise. A person is *identified as multidimensionally poor* if the person's count of deprivations is greater than some specified cutoff (k):

if $c_i \geq k$, then $q_i = 1$

if $c_i < k$, then $q_i = 0$

The *headcount ratio* for a given population is then the number of poor persons ($q = \Sigma q_i$) divided by the total population (n):

$$H = \frac{q}{n} \tag{5.1}$$

To capture the breadth of deprivations experienced by the multidimensionally poor, in other words, the experience of deprivation in several dimensions, the average number of deprivations that a multidimensionally poor person faces is computed. The total number of deprivations experienced by multidimensionally poor people $c(k)$ is calculated as follows: $c(k) = \Sigma(q_i c_i)$ for i = 1...n. The ***average deprivation share*** is the total number of deprivations of the disadvantaged ($c(k)$) divided by the maximum number of deprivations that the deprived could face (qd):

$$A = \frac{c(k)}{qd} \tag{5.2}$$

The ***adjusted headcount ratio,*** M_0, combines information on the prevalence of multidimensional poverty and its breadth, as the product of the headcount ratio and average deprivation share:

$$M_0 = HA = \frac{c(k)}{nd} \tag{5.3}$$

It is important to note that this method has a number of limitations. First, the three measures above are a function of the weights allocated arbitrarily to dimensions. Thus, any poverty calculation using this framework is sensitive to the assumptions used in setting weights. Second, this method is sensitive to the selection of dimensions, and there is no guidance on how to select them. Furthermore, this method also requires that a cutoff is set for each dimension/indicator. Deciding on a specific cutoff point is an arbitrary choice, although it can be an informed one. The cutoff across dimensions—the share of dimensions whereby one needs to experience deprivation—also needs to be specified. As noted in Alkire and Foster (2011), setting the cutoff points 'establishes the minimum eligibility criteria for poverty in terms of breadth of deprivation and reflects a judgment regarding the maximally acceptable multiplicity of deprivations' (p. 483). This judgment is based on expert opinion and seems particularly difficult to make in a cross-country study such as this one. Since multidimensional poverty measures require assumptions for the selection of dimensions, weights, and thresholds, these assumptions are described in detail below.

Based on the information available in the datasets above and the guidance of Stiglitz et al. (2009), five dimensions were selected for the calculation of the multidimensional poverty measure as presented in Table 5.2. The five dimensions include three dimensions of individual wellbeing—education, health and personal activities (work)—and two dimensions at the household level material wellbeing and economic

Table 5.2 Dimensions, indicators and weights in the multidimensional poverty measure

Dimension	*Indicator(s)*	*Threshold: Deprived if…*	*Dimension Weight*	*Indicator Weight*
Education			1/5	
	Educational attainment	Individual has less than primary schooling		1/5
Health			1/5	
	Morbidity	Individual suffered from an illness or injury recently		1/5
Personal activities			1/5	
	Work status	Individual is not working		1/5
Material wellbeing			1/5	
	Sanitation	The household's sanitation facility is not improved, or it is improved but shared with other households.		1/30
	Water	The household does not have access to safe drinking water or safe drinking water is more than a 30-min walk from home, round trip.		1/30
	Cooking fuel	The household cooks with dung, wood, or charcoal.		1/30
	Electricity	The household has no electricity.		1/30
	Flooring	The household has a dirt, sand, or dung floor.		1/30
	Assets	The household does not own more than one asset (among radio, TV, telephone, bike, motorbike, or refrigerator) and does not own a car or truck.		1/30
Insecurity			1/5	
	Food insecurity	In the past 12 months, household respondent was faced with a situation where did not have enough food to feed the household.		1/10
	Shock	Household experienced at least one shock in the past 12 months.		1/10

Notes 3, 4 and 5 of Table 5.1 apply

insecurity. In the context of the human development model, the multidimensional poverty measures capture deprivations in terms of functionings, not capabilities. These functionings are related to material wellbeing, economic security, education, morbidity, and work (Fig. 3.1).

The five dimensions are equally weighted and when more than one indicator is used within a dimension, indicators are equally weighted within the dimension. An individual is identified as multidimensionally poor if he or she is deprived in some combination of indicators whose weighted sum exceeds 40%.

The within dimension indicator cutoffs are given in Table 5.2. The selection of indicators and cutoffs was based on a review of the literature measuring the wellbeing dimensions above. As shown in Table 5.2, for household material wellbeing, six indicators are used for assets and living conditions similar to Alkire and Santos (2010), and for household insecurity, two indicators are used: food insecurity and exposure to a shock.[11] Each of the other dimensions uses only one indicator. The cutoffs for the indicators are as follows: if a person (1) has less than primary schooling; (2) has been sick or injured recently; (3) does not work; (4) The household's sanitation facility is not improved, or it is improved but shared with other households; (5) The household does not have access to safe drinking water or safe drinking water is more than a 30-min walk from home, roundtrip; (6) The household cooks with dung, wood, or charcoal; (7) The household has no electricity; (8) The household has a dirt, sand, or dung floor; (9) The household does not own more than one asset (among radio, TV, telephone, bike, motorbike, or refrigerator) and does not own a car or truck; (10) In the past 12 months, household respondent faced with a situation when did not have enough food to feed the household; (11) Household experienced at least one shock in the past 12 months. One could argue that some of the thresholds may not capture deprivations. For instance, not working is considered as a deprivation while it may not be, if no or limited decent work is available.

For each of the wellbeing indicators described above, descriptive statistics are presented and include cross-tabulations for each indicator across functional difficulty status. Multivariate regression analysis is also used.

5.2.2.1 Multivariate Analysis

A linear relationship is specified in which a wellbeing indicator is a function of functional difficulties, individual, household, and community characteristics. For each of the individual wellbeing indicators in Table 5.1 and the multidimensional poverty status described above, a model is used as described in Box 3.

Box 3: Multivariate regression of wellbeing

An OLS or a logistic regression is run in turn for individual wellbeing outcomes as follows:

$$IndivWellbeing_i = \alpha + \beta_1 Severe_i + \beta_2 Moderate_i + \sum_k \gamma_k x_{i,k} + \varepsilon_i \qquad (5.4)$$

where

- *IndivWellbeing*$_i$ is an individual wellbeing outcome for person i which is in turn: ever attended school, sick or injured in the past month, work and work hours (definitions are in Table 5.1).
- α is the intercept;
- *Severe*$_i$ is a variable equal to 1 if individual i has a severe functional difficulty, 0 otherwise;
- *Moderate*$_i$ is a dummy variable equal to 1 if individual i has a moderate functional difficulty, 0 otherwise;
- β_1 and β_2 are the coefficients of the functional difficulty variables, to be estimated;

They are the coefficients of interest and their values are reported for each country in Table 5.4.

- $x_{i,k}$ is a set of k control variables for personal factors (age categories, male), resources and structural factors (being married, being the household head, having a mother with no prior schooling, household size, distance to healthcare).[12]
- γ_k are the estimated coefficients for the set of k control variables but are not reported in Table 5.4.
- ε_i is the error term for person *i*.

In a variant of (5.4), the functional difficulty variables are replaced by the functional score defined earlier in Chapter 3.

For each of the household wellbeing indicators in Table 5.1, a similar regression model as (5.4) above is estimated:

$$HHWellbeing_i = \alpha + \beta_1 Severe_i + \beta_2 Moderate_i + \sum_k \gamma_k x_{i,k} + \varepsilon_i \tag{5.5}$$

where

HHWellbeing$_i$ is a household wellbeing outcome for household i which is in turn is: asset score, below the $1.90 per day poverty line, total expenditures, total expenditures (nonhealth), education expenditures, health expenditures, social protection transfers, food insecurity, shocks (definitions are in Table 5.1).

Other symbols are as above for (5.4) except for the set of control variables at the household level (household head's age, marital status, educational attainment, household size, shares of members under age 15 and over age 60, share of male members[13]) and the community level (rural, distance to healthcare services).

It is essential to note that the models above suffer from several important limitations. The first limitation deals with multicollinearity in each of the models. In other words, the control variables are themselves interrelated. As shown in Chapter 4, functional status is related to age, gender, and rural residence.[14] This, on the other hand, may lead to biased estimates of the coefficient of the functional status variables in the regressions. More importantly, the above models suffer from omitted variable bias. For instance, they do not control for potential confounders, which can affect both wellbeing indicators and functional status. Possible confounders include, for example, violence in the community or household, community services (e.g., health and education facilities, roads), which could affect both functional status and wellbeing indicators. The community control variables (rural residence, distance to healthcare services) in (5.4) and (5.5) above are a very crude way to adjust for these potential structural factors at the community level that may impact household or individual wellbeing as well as functional difficulties.

5.3 Results and Discussion

Results are presented in a set of tables and graphs using the data described in Chapter 3 starting with individual, then household wellbeing and finally multidimensional poverty.

5.3.1 Individual Wellbeing

Table 5.3 compares individual outcomes for persons with severe, moderate, or no difficulty for all adults, and then separately for women and men. In all four countries, individuals with moderate or severe functional difficulty have less often ever been to school and are more likely to have been sick or injured recently. The gap in educational attainment across functional difficulty status is large in the four countries. For instance, in Ethiopia, only 15% and 24% of persons with severe and moderate difficulties, respectively, have ever attended school compared to 48% of persons with no difficulty.

The gap in morbidity is large in Ethiopia, Malawi, and Uganda but not in Tanzania. This likely results from the different measures used in Tanzania which is healthcare use and not morbidity.

Individuals with severe difficulties in all four countries are less likely to be working and have fewer work hours than persons with no difficulty. There is a large gap in employment rates in all four countries between persons with severe and no difficulty. The largest is in Tanzania where 53% of persons with severe difficulties work, compared to 85.4% among persons without any difficulty. This result of a consistent gap in employment rates for severe functional difficulty stands in contrast to the results in Mizunoya and Mitra (2013) which found a significant gap in only two out of eight LICs using a measure of severe functional difficulty in seeing, moving, concentrating, or selfcare. For moderate difficulty, a significantly lower employment rate is found in Uganda only and significantly lower work hours are found in Ethiopia, Tanzania, and Uganda.

Regarding work type, persons with severe difficulties are less likely to be in wage work and more likely to do household business work in three out of four countries. There is no consistent pattern for farm work with persons with functional difficulties less often in farm work in Ethiopia and Malawi, more often in Tanzania. No significant difference is found in Uganda.

Table 5.3 Individual wellbeing outcomes by functional status

	Ethiopia			*Malawi*			*Tanzania*			*Uganda*		
	Severe	*Moderate*	*None*	*Severe*	*Moderate*	*None*	*Severe*	*Moderate*	*None*	*Severe*	*Moderate*	*None*
All adults												
Ever attended school	0.15***	0.24***	0.48	0.48***	0.68***	0.81	0.42***	0.65***	0.80	0.60***	0.73***	0.89
Sick or injured in past month	0.57***	0.39***	0.17	0.38***	0.31***	0.14	0.19**	0.20***	0.15	0.68***	0.65***	0.37
Work	0.55***	0.75	0.75	0.62***	0.81	0.81	0.53***	0.84	0.85	0.56***	0.89***	0.89
Work hours per week	28.23***	32.06**	33.91	15.88***	20.49	21.05	20.92***	25.88**	27.82	18.58***	23.35***	29.47
Type of work:												
Household farm work	0.67***	0.70**	0.73	0.58***	0.63	0.61	0.73**	0.70**	0.65	0.61	0.64	0.61
Household business work	0.26**	0.23*	0.21	0.06**	0.09	0.10	0.13	0.14	0.14	0.27***	0.22***	0.20
Wage work	0.00**	0.01	0.01	0.08**	0.09**	0.11	0.07***	0.09***	0.14	0.13***	0.14***	0.19
Other work	0.06	0.06	0.05	0.28***	0.19	0.18	0.07	0.07	0.07	0	0	0
Women												
Ever attended school	0.14***	0.15***	0.37	0.35***	0.60***	0.75	0.30***	0.57***	0.74	0.48***	0.63***	0.84
Sick or injured in past month	0.56***	0.42***	0.19	0.41***	0.33***	0.16	0.23	0.23***	0.18	0.76***	0.69***	0.42
Work	0.50***	0.68	0.68	0.60***	0.78	0.78	0.54***	0.81	0.83	0.51***	0.88***	0.80
Work hours per week	25.55***	29.75	31.75	12.43***	17.83**	17.64	17.65***	21.71*	23.81	19.32***	22.02***	26.86

(continued)

Table 5.3 (continued)

	Ethiopia			*Malawi*			*Tanzania*			*Uganda*		
	Severe	*Moderate*	*None*	*Severe*	*Moderate*	*None*	*Severe*	*Moderate*	*None*	*Severe*	*Moderate*	*None*
Type of work:												
Household farm work	0.53	0.59	0.63	0.65	0.67	0.68	0.70***	0.68*	0.70	0.72	0.71	0.69
Household business work	0.46	0.35	0.31	0.03*	0.09	0.09	0.14	0.17***	0.11	0.23**	0.18**	0.18
Wage work	0.00	0.01	0.01	0.02	0.05	0.04	0.05	0.06*	0.08	0.50**	0.10	0.12
Other work	0.02	0.06	0.05	0.30***	0.19	0.19	0.09	0.09	0.10	0.00	0.00	0.00
Men												
Ever attended school	0.16***	0.33***	0.59	0.65***	0.81***	0.87	0.61***	0.74***	0.86	0.74***	0.87***	0.94
Sick or injured recently	0.59***	0.36***	0.15	0.34***	0.27***	0.12	0.14***	0.17***	0.11	0.60***	0.61***	0.32
Work	0.61***	0.82	0.82	0.63***	0.84*	0.84	0.51***	0.88	0.88	0.60***	0.89	0.86
Work hours per week	30.57***	34.08*	35.71	20.14**	24.10	24.22	26.30*	30.66	32.56	17.76***	25.10***	32.05
Type of work:												
Household farm work	0.81***	0.80*	0.81	0.49	0.59***	0.54	0.75***	0.72***	0.59	0.50	0.54	0.52
Household business work	0.09**	0.13**	0.13	0.10	0.09	0.10	0.11	0.10 ***	0.18	0.30	0.27***	0.21
Wage work	0.00	0.01	0.02	0.15	0.14**	0.17	0.12*	0.14**	0.20	0.20*	0.19***	0.26
Other work	0.10	0.06	0.05	0.26	0.18	0.19	0.02	0.04	0.04	0	0	0.01

Notes ***significant at the 1% level, **significant at the 5% level, *significant at the 10% level for the difference with individuals with no difficulty. More information on the wellbeing indicators is in Table 5.1. Statistical significance is tested with ttest for continuous variable and the Pearson's Chi square test for binary variables. Estimates are weighted

Table 5.4 Regressions of individual outcomes on functional difficulty status and other covariates

	Ethiopia		*Malawi*		*Tanzania*		*Uganda*	
	Severe	*Moderate*	*Severe*	*Moderate*	*Severe*	*Moderate*	*Severe*	*Moderate*
All adults								
Ever attended school	0.39***	0.84*	0.71**	1.20***	0.59***	1.07	0.46***	0.85*
Sick or injured in past month	4.76***	2.46***	3.00***	2.16***	1.37*	1.38***	2.80***	2.20***
Work	0.42***	1.00	0.28***	0.79***	0.19***	0.67***	0.25***	1.17
Work hours	−6.21***	−3.15**	−5.18***	0.57	−4.80*	−0.40	−6.00***	−4.50***
Women								
Ever attended school	0.60	0.80	0.57***	1.18***	0.66	1.06	0.74	0.99
Sick or injured in past month	4.03***	2.42***	2.31***	2.04***	1.36	1.34**	3.50***	2.09***
Work	0.45***	0.95	0.37***	0.85**	0.36***	0.93**	0.30***	1.35*
Work hours	−7.14***	−2.41	−4.22***	0.64	−6.70***	−1.48	3.30	−3.28**
Men								
Ever attended school	0.33***	0.87	0.89	1.32**	0.66*	0.83	0.26***	0.73
Sick or injured in past month	5.66***	2.52***	3.19***	2.30***	1.47	1.51***	2.37***	2.20***
Work	0.39***	1.11	0.19***	0.62***	0.09***	0.49***	0.21***	0.86
Work hours	−5.36**	−3.74*	−6.42***	0.43	−3.12	−1.77	−8.96***	−6.12***

Notes For each wellbeing indicator in a given row, a multivariate regression is run and the coefficients of moderate difficulty and severe difficulty dummies are reported on the same row. No functional difficulty is the reference category. All regressions are run as logistic regressions except for work hours run as OLS. Coefficients are then odds ratios except for work hours. ***significant at the 1% level, **significant at the 5% level, *significant at the 10% level. More information on the dependent variables is in Table 5.1. Descriptive statistics are in Table 5.3 for the dependent variables and in Table 4.4 for control variables. The regression controls are as follows: age categories, sex (for the entire sample of all adults), being married, being the household head, having a mother with no prior schooling, household size, rural and distance to healthcare services. For Tanzania, data was missing for distance to healthcare services for a sizeable share of the sample, community fixed effects were used instead

These results above largely hold in subsamples of women and men in the bottom two panels of Table 5.3. Comparing now women to men, women are less likely to have ever been to school, more likely to have been sick or injured recently and less likely to work, whatever the functional difficulty status.

Perhaps these results so far reflect to some extent cohort effects, with persons with functional difficulties being on average older and having less education. The association between functional difficulty and deprivations at the individual level is further considered through the regression model (5.4) of Box 3 controlling for various characteristics, including age. As shown in Table 5.4, results are quite consistent across countries. Moderate and severe difficulties are significantly associated with lower odds of ever attending school and higher odds of being sick or injured. For work, lower odds of working and lower hours of work are associated with severe difficulty in all countries. For instance, in Uganda, the odds of working for a person with a severe difficulty are 0.25 the odds of working of a person with no functional difficulty, everything else equal. Results are more mixed for moderate difficulty with a significant association with lower odds of working in Malawi and Tanzania, and significantly lower work hours in Ethiopia, Tanzania, and Uganda.

Similar regressions are run with the individual functional difficulty score in Table 5.5 instead of the severe and moderate difficulty binary variables. The functional difficulty score is consistently and significantly associated with worse individual wellbeing outcomes for all country–indicator pair except schooling in Malawi. For example, in Ethiopia, a 10% higher functional score is associated with a 32.7% lower probability of working.

Table 5.5 Regressions of individual outcomes on functional score and other covariates

	Ethiopia	*Malawi*	*Tanzania*	*Uganda*
Ever attended school	−4.13***	0.37	−1.59***	−3.35***
Sick or injured in past month	7.06***	7.37***	2.15***	5.69***
Work	−3.27***	−5.47***	−5.82***	−5.84***
Work hours	−36.08***	−11.65**	−18.08**	−37.48***

Note The notes of Table 5.4 apply. The right hand side variable of interest for which the estimated coefficient is reported is the functional score.

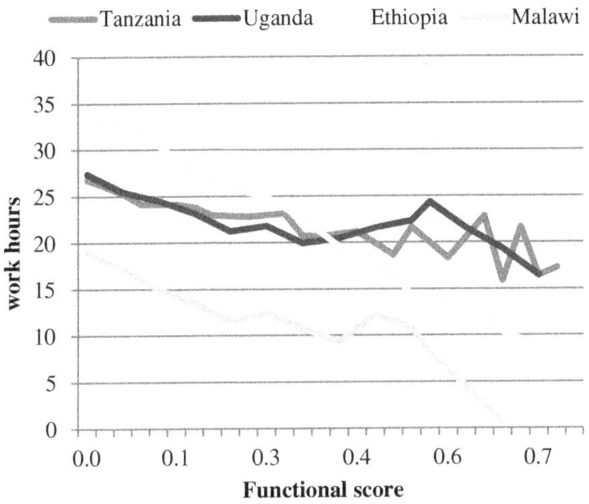

Fig. 5.1 Predicted work hours by functional score

Notes This is the predicted mean work hours by functional score among working adults using an OLS regression with control variables as follows: age categories, sex, being married, being the household head, having a mother with no prior schooling, household size and distance to healthcare services

Figure 5.1 gives the predicted value of work hours vs. the individual functional score, based on the regression model in Table 5.5. For all four countries, there is a negative relationship between work hours and functional score, which extends from low to high values of the functional score. It also applies to values of the functional score in the moderate difficulty range, for example from 0.05 to 0.10. There is a gradient in work hours across severe, moderate, and no difficulty.

5.3.2 Household Wellbeing

Table 5.6 compares wellbeing outcomes of households with at least an adult with a severe or moderate difficulty to households with no functional difficulty. In all four countries, households with an adult with a moderate or severe functional difficulty tend to have worse living conditions or own fewer assets as reflected by a lower asset score. They are also more prone to economic insecurity with higher shares of food insecure households and households subject to a recent shock.

Table 5.6 Household wellbeing outcomes by functional status (means unless otherwise noted)

	E thiopia			*Malawi*		
	Severe	*Moderate*	*None*	*Severe*	*Moderate*	*None*
Asset index	13.76***	14.72**	15.81	11.22***	14.9	15.14
	(0.82)	(0.61)	(0.33)	(0.59)	(0.40)	(0.20)
Share of households below $1.90 per day	NA	NA	NA	0.64***	0.52	0.53
Total expenditures	NA	NA	NA	191,601.30	250,328.10	248,146.80
				(9,201.33)	(9,824.46)	(4,370.98)
Total exp. (nonhealth)	NA	NA	NA	187,078.50 *	246,508.10	245,031.60
				(19,046.16)	(18,733.02)	(14,314.64)
Health exp.	NA	NA	NA	4,572.80***	3,820.06***	3,115.10
				(720.16)	(285.56)	(235.62)
Education expenditures	91.39**	182.49	168.40	3,019.83	7,419.06**	5,588.35
	(14.94)	(18.23)	(14.15)	(458.19)	(1,126.22)	(411.64)
Social transfers	62.68	47.69 *	29.59	477.13	328.46	575.13
	(15.28)	(13.26)	(10.65)	(349.82)	(129.57)	(267.50)
Share of food insecure households	0.19***	0.21***	0.16	0.43***	0.34***	0.30
Share of households subject to a shock recently	0.55***	0.59***	0.48	0.76***	0.69***	0.65

(continued)

Table 5.6 (continued)

	Tanzania			*Uganda*		
	Severe	*Moderate*	*None*	*Severe*	*Moderate*	*None*
Asset index	16.82***	23.02***	25.33	28.24***	29.67***	33.25
	(1.28)	(0.91)	(0.62)	(1.02)	(0.88)	(0.59)
Share of households below $1.90 per day	0.20***	0.12	0.12	0.57*	0.46	0.45
Total expenditures	2,036,795.00***	2,876,496.00*	2,690,722.00	257,213.20	267,776.90	263,203.80
	(1142,123.40)	(1133,625.50)	(168,999.53)	(19523.56)	(14086.71)	(8961.32)
Total exp. (nonhealth)	1,930,099.00***	2,759,560.00	2,599,069.00	256,764.70	267,365.50	262,806.50
	(1137,693.70)	(1128,816.40)	(1066,860.65)	(19518.04)	(14084.40)	(8959.48)
Health exp.	106,696.50**	116,935.70**	91,653.09	448.45**	411.38**	397.36
	(116,281.18)	(113,066.96)	(16,191.04)	(18.82)	(14.04)	(9.61)
Education exp.	84,097.38	207,056.70*	133,104.90	375,679.30	370,427.90**	295,928.70
	(22586.38)	(28159.92)	(13075.30)	(79736.80)	(47387.87)	(26629.60)
Social transfers	1,525.19***	372.59	309.62	NA	NA	NA
	(623.87)	(113.86)	(59.63)			
Share of food insecure households	0.42***	0.43***	0.32	0.34***	0.30**	0.18
Share of households subject to a shock recently	0.88*	0.88***	0.80	0.56***	0.48***	0.37

Notes Table includes sample means and standard errors (between brackets) for household indicators of Table 5.1. NA stands for not available. Estimates are weighted. Expenditures and tranfers are in domestic currencies (Birrs for Ethiopia, Kwachas for Malawi, Tanzania Shillings for Tanzania, Uganda Shillings for Uganda). 1) exp. stands for expenditures 2) Social transfers stands for Social protection transfers

The poverty headcount using the $1.90 a day poverty line is about 10 percentage point higher among households with severe functional difficulties in Malawi, Tanzania, and Uganda. No significant difference is found for households with moderate difficulties. Mean total expenditures and total nonhealth expenditures are not significantly different across groups except in Tanzania where they are significantly lower among households with severe difficulties. Households with functional difficulties incur significantly higher health expenditures than other households in Malawi and Tanzania, but not in Uganda. In Ethiopia, significantly lower educational expenditures are found, but not in other countries. Households with functional difficulties receive significantly higher social protection transfers in Tanzania, but not in Ethiopia and Malawi.

This association between household economic indicators and functional difficulties may be due to differences in household characteristics. Perhaps the lower education expenditures found in Ethiopia for households with a severe functional difficulty result from the older ages of household members when a household has a severe functional difficulty. The associations are analyzed further in Table 5.7 with multivariate regressions. It gives the estimated coefficient of the two variables that indicate if at least one adult in the household experiences a severe or moderate functional difficulty. The model includes as controls the household head and household characteristics described in Box 3 and Table 4.7.

In the four countries, households with functional difficulties, whether moderate or severe, are consistently more likely to be food insecure and to experience a shock. For instance, in Uganda, households with moderate or severe functional difficulties, respectively, have 1.3 or 1.8 higher odds of being subject to shocks than households without any functional difficulty.

For other household outcomes, results vary across countries. Having an adult with a functional difficulty in the household is significantly associated with lower asset ownership in Ethiopia and Tanzania, lower total expenditures in Tanzania, lower education expenditures in Ethiopia and Malawi and higher health expenditures in two out of three countries (Malawi and Tanzania). It is significantly correlated with higher social protection transfers in Ethiopia, Malawi, and Tanzania for moderate or severe functional difficulties.

Total expenditures do not differ across functional status in all countries, except for moderate functional difficulty in Malawi. This is consistent with Mitra et al. (2013), who, based on a bivariate analysis, find no significant difference in expenditures in 15 LMICs using WHS data,

Table 5.7 Regressions of household wellbeing outcomes on severe and moderate functional difficulties and other covariates

	Ethiopia		*Malawi*		*Tanzania*		*Uganda*	
	Severe	*Moderate*	*Severe*	*Moderate*	*Severe*	*Moderate*	*Severe*	*Moderate*
Asset index	13.76***	−0.85	0.83	0.67	−3.39***	−2.11**	−0.76	−0.60
Below $1.90 per day	NA	NA	1.18	0.88*	1.14	1.23	0.89	1.18
Total expenditures	NA	NA	−0.02	0.04**	−0.04	0.01	0.01	0.02
Total expenditures (nonhealth)	NA	NA	−0.03	0.03*	−0.07	0.00	0.01	0.02
Health expenditures	NA	NA	0.82***	0.87***	1.09***	0.67**	0.20	0.00
Education expenditures	−0.49***	0.04	−0.56***	0.10	0.58	0.12	−0.18	−0.27
Social protection transfers	0.33***	0.11	0.04	0.13***	0.29**	0.07	NA	NA
Food insecurity	1.64***	1.30**	1.59***	1.20***	1.57**	1.80***	1.83**	1.29*
Shocks	1.50***	1.45***	1.51***	1.28***	1.39	2.10***	1.42**	1.29**

Notes Each row for each country gives the estimated coefficients of the household moderate and severe functional difficulty binary variables in a regression of a household wellbeing outcome. No functional difficulty is the reference category. The dependent variable is the row header (e.g. asset index). All expenditures variables are logged. For continuous dependent variables (asset index, expenditure variables, social protection transfers) the coefficients are from an OLS regression. For binary dependent variables (below $1.90 a day, food insecurity and household subject to shocks in the past year), the coefficients are odds ratios from a logistic regression. ***significant at the 1% level, **significant at the 5% level, *significant at the 10% level. NA stands for not available. Descriptive statistics for all variables are in Table 4.7 and 5.6. The regression controls are as follows: household head's age, marital status, educational attainment, household size, share of members under age 15 and over age 60, share of male members, rural and distance to healthcare services. For Tanzania, data was missing for distance to healthcare services for a sizable share of the sample, community fixed effects were used instead

where the expenditures survey questions were few and not detailed. Using a very detailed expenditure questionnaire from the LSMS, no significant difference is found here either.

Some differences are found though for certain types of expenditures. Health expenditures information is available in three countries. Having a moderate or severe functional difficulty is associated with higher health expenditures in Malawi and Tanzania but not for Uganda. This result supports the hypothesis of conversion factors associated with functional difficulty as explained in Chapter 2. Households with functional difficulties have on average higher health expenditures in Malawi and Tanzania, which may make the conversion of income into wellbeing more challenging. In particular, higher health expenditures may crowd out other expenditures and indirectly make households more prone to worse living conditions, asset accumulation and food insecurity as shown earlier.

Significantly lower education expenditures are associated with a severe functional difficulty in Ethiopia and Malawi, but not in Tanzania and Uganda. This might suggest an allocation of expenditures away from education and toward health or other expenditures affected by the functional difficulty as found in Mitra et al. (2016) for Vietnam.

In the four countries, a consistent result is that having a moderate difficulty is less strongly associated with a household wellbeing deprivation than having a severe difficulty across all household wellbeing indicators. Nonetheless, households with a moderate difficulty are more often deprived, everything else held constant, than households with no functional difficulty especially with respect to food insecurity and shocks.

Similar regressions are run with the household functional difficulty score[15] in Table 5.8 instead of the severe and moderate difficulty binary variables in Table 5.7. The functional difficulty score is associated with worse household wellbeing outcomes for three to five wellbeing indicators by country. For instance, for a household in Ethiopia, a 10% higher functional difficulty score is associated with 13.4% higher odds of having experienced a recent shock and 11.2% higher odds of being food insecure. It is also associated with education expenditures lower by 16.3 ETB (Ethiopian Birr) and social protection transfers higher by 10.2 ETB.

5.3.2.1 Multidimensional Poverty

Results of the multidimensional poverty analysis using Alkire and Foster (2011) and the dimensions, indicators and weights in Table 5.2 are first shown in the spider charts in Fig. 5.2, which gives the deprivation rates across functional difficulty status for each of the five dimensions.

Table 5.8 Regressions of household wellbeing outcomes on functional score and other covariates

	Ethiopia	*Malawi*	*Tanzania*	*Uganda*
Asset index	−3.61	−0.03	−13.1***	−6.70**
Below $1.90 per day	NA	1.08	1.28	2.53
Total expenditures	NA	−0.03	−0.05	0.00
Total expenditures (nonhealth)	NA	−0.10	−1.16	−0.01
Health expenditures	NA	6.42***	4.81***	0.15
Education expenditures	−1.63***	−1.52**	−1.63***	−0.58
Social protection transfers	1.02***	1.05***	0.66	0.66
Food insecurity	1.12*	2.87***	2.04***	0.52***
Shocks	1.34***	2.11***	1.73**	0.36*

Notes Each row for each country gives the estimated coefficient of the household functional score in a regression of a household wellbeing outcome. Other notes on dependent and independent variables of Table 5.7 apply. NA stands for not available

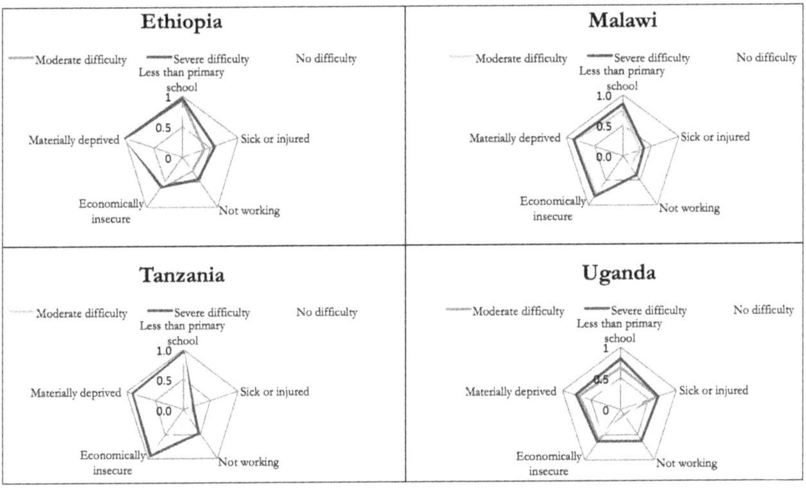

Fig. 5.2 Rates of deprivation by dimension and functional difficulty status. *Note* Deprivations using dimensions, thresholds and indicators described in Table 5.2

The three lines, from dark to light green, connect the deprivation rates for persons with severe, moderate, or no difficulty, respectively. Unsurprisingly, the darker lines are on the outskirts of the lighter line for each country, showing higher deprivation rates for persons with functional difficulties. The gaps between the lines are larger for individual wellbeing dimensions (less than primary school, sick or injured and not working) than for household wellbeing dimensions (materially deprived and economically insecure). The gap between persons with moderate and no difficulty is smaller than the gap between persons with severe and no difficulty.

Results for multidimensional poverty measures are given in Fig. 5.3 and Appendix A4 for all adults. A higher headcount (H) is found among persons with moderate or severe functional difficulties, and the difference across functional difficulty status is found to be statistically significant in all countries. More than eight in 10 adults with functional difficulties experience multidimensional poverty. Roughly, the difference in the multidimensional headcount ratio is around 20 and 10 percentage points in the four countries comparing, respectively, persons with severe and moderate difficulties to persons without any difficulty.

The average deprivation share (A), i.e. the share of dimensions in which the poor have deprivations, is significantly higher among persons with severe or moderate difficulty in all countries (Appendix A4). In other words, the poor with functional difficulties face more deprivations than the poor without any functional difficulty. Appendix A4 also presents the adjusted headcount ratio (M_0). The adjusted headcount ratio is found to be higher among persons with functional difficulties than persons without in all countries. The difference in the adjusted headcount ratio across functional difficulty status is the largest in Uganda; it is more than twice higher among persons with severe functional difficulties compared to persons without any difficulty. The gaps across functional difficulty status found in almost all dimensions of wellbeing earlier in Fig. 5.2 suggest that the gaps also found with multidimensional poverty measures are not sensitive to the dimension weights used in the analysis (Table 5.2).

Appendix A5 gives multidimensional poverty measures for sex and age subgroups. While women almost always have higher multidimensional poverty than men whatever the functional difficulty status, women with functional difficulties also have higher H, A and M_0 than women without difficulties. It shows that women with functional difficulties experience

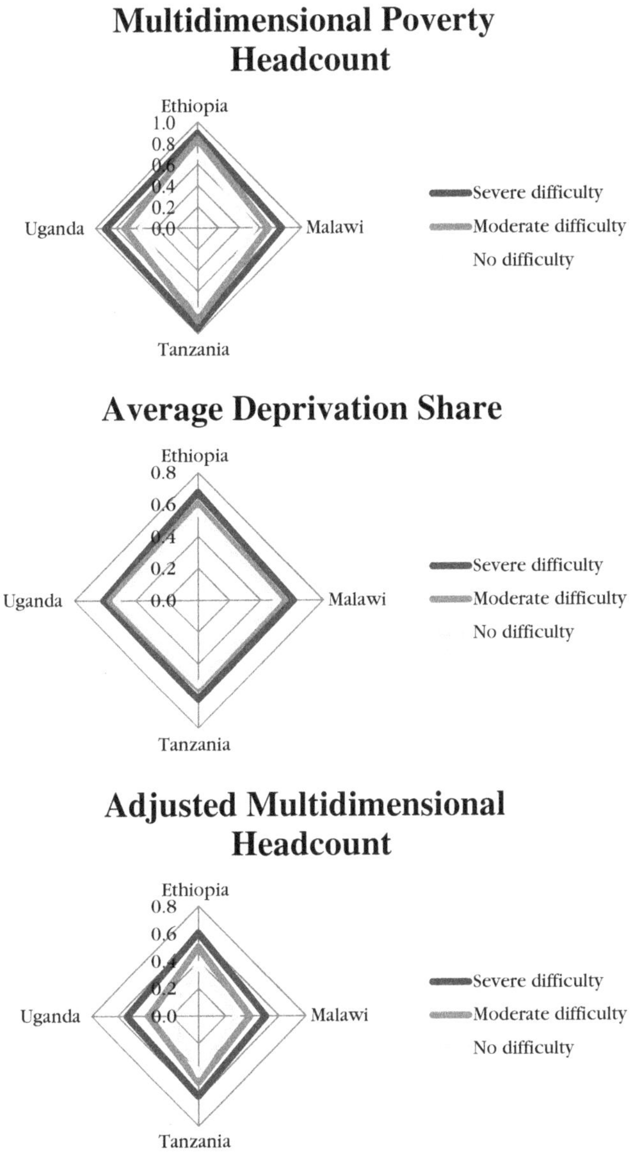

Fig. 5.3 Multidimensional poverty and functional difficulty status

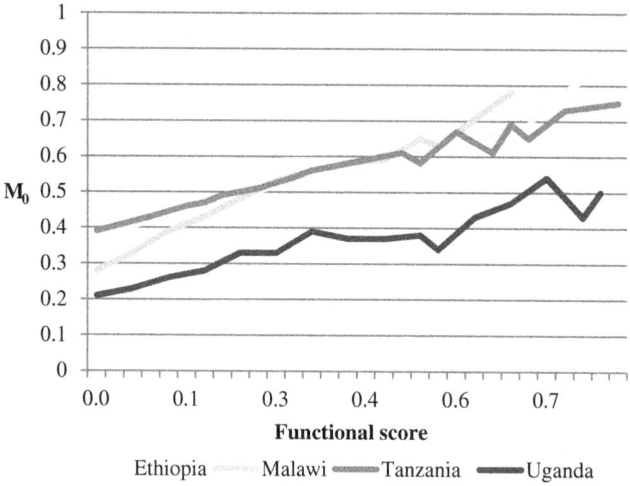

Fig. 5.4 Predicted multidimensional poverty adjusted headcount (M_0) by functional score. *Note* This is the mean adjusted multidimensional headcount by functional score using an OLS regression as in Box 3

a double disadvantage associated with gender and functional difficulty. This double disadvantage is, for instance, stark in Uganda where 96% of women with severe functional difficulties are multidimensionally poor compared to 52% of men with no functional difficulty. By age group, the assessment is somewhat different. Among persons with no functional difficulty, being older than 50 is not always associated with being more often multidimensionally poor than those younger than 50; for H, it is the case in Ethiopia and Malawi, but not in Tanzania and Uganda. However, having a functional difficulty is consistently associated with being more often multidimensionally poor within each age group.

Figure 5.4 gives the predicted M_0 by functional score after adjusting for a number of covariates listed in Box 3. In the four countries, there is a positive and steep gradient in the functional score. Appendix A6 gives the full results of the regression. The functional difficulty score is the covariate with the highest coefficient, above those of sex, age groups, marital status, mother's schooling, rural residence, and the distance to healthcare services.

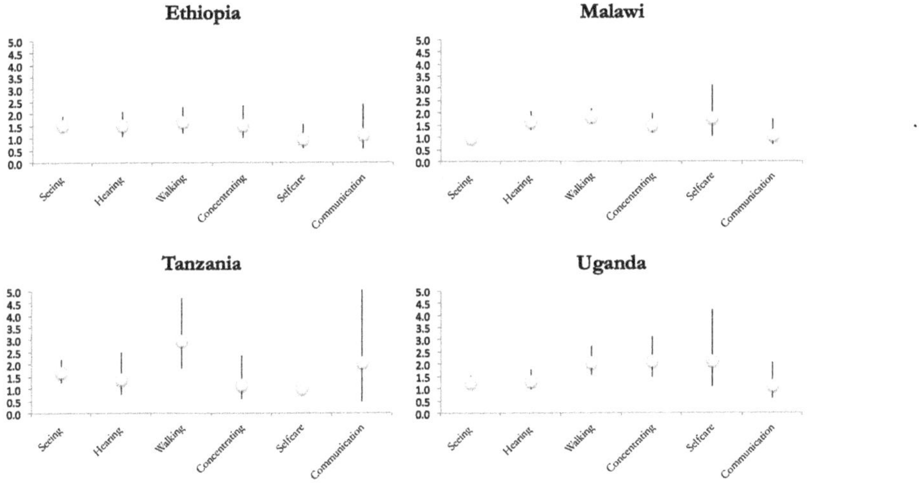

Fig. 5.5 Odds ratio of being multi-dimensionally poor by type of functional difficulty

5.3.2.2 Type of Functional Limitation and Age of Onset

Finally, Fig. 5.5 presents results of a logistic regression of the probability of being multidimensionally poor. It gives the odds ratio of being multidimensionally poor for each functional difficulty type among all adults. For instance, for seeing in Malawi, an odds ratio close to one indicates that having this difficulty is associated with odds of being multidimensionally poor that are similar to those of a person without such difficulty, everything else held constant. A lower bound of the confidence interval above one for the odds ratio indicates a higher likelihood of being multidimensionally poor associated with a functional difficulty type. Figure 5.5 shows that having a walking difficulty is associated with higher odds of being multidimensionally poor in all four countries, followed by having a concentrating difficulty in three countries and a seeing, hearing, or selfcare difficulty in two countries, and communication difficulty in no country.

While Fig. 5.5 is focused on multidimensional poverty, Appendix A7 considers in turn a deprivation in a domain (e.g., education, morbidity) and its association with the different functional disability types among all adults. Results are consistent with those in Fig. 5.5, with walking as the functional difficulty the most often associated with deprivations.

Finally, for Tanzania and Uganda, information is available on age at onset among persons with functional difficulties as shown earlier in Fig. 4.3. The model of Box 3 was used this time replacing moderate and severe functional difficulties with age at onset during working age years (15–49 years old) and age at onset during old age (50 and above). The sample was restricted to persons with functional difficulties. Results are not shown. Having an onset from birth to age 14 was the reference category. Among persons with functional limitations, no significant association was found between having an onset during working age or older years and having different odds of deprivation in turn for each wellbeing domain (e.g., education, morbidity) and for multidimensional poverty. The exception was for Tanzania, where having an onset during working age years was significantly associated with higher odds of being materially deprived.

5.4 Conclusion: Summary and Implications

The results in this chapter add to a small but growing quantitative literature on the association between disability and inequalities by using an internationally comparable disability measure and very detailed economic wellbeing information. Compared to earlier studies, it has indeed more detailed information on employment, household expenditures, and economic insecurity. I summarize below the main results of interest of this chapter and derive policy and research implications.

1. Results from both descriptive statistics and regressions indicate that functional difficulties, whether moderate or severe, are significant and large correlates of both individual and household wellbeing deprivations in Ethiopia, Malawi, Tanzania, and Uganda. This is found through an indicator-by-indicator analysis as well as through an assessment of multidimensional poverty, in descriptive and multivariate analyses. More than eight in ten persons with severe functional difficulties experience multidimensional poverty in Ethiopia, Malawi, Tanzania, and Uganda.
2. The association is found to be strong and consistent for several dimensions of wellbeing at both the individual (education, morbidity, work status) and the household levels (economic insecurity).

The association seems stronger and more consistent than in earlier studies (e.g., Filmer 2008; Mitra et al. 2013; Trani et al. 2015).

These results support the inclusion of moderate and severe functional difficulties as potential correlates of deprivations in poverty monitoring, evaluation, and programmatic efforts in LMICs. It also supports a disaggregation by functional difficulty status of the indicators used to monitor the SDGs, in particular SDG #1, which states as a goal the eradication of hunger and poverty 'in all its forms' (UNDP 2016).

The result on household-level economic insecurity is consistent with results from qualitative research that deprivations are not contained to the individual and are also a 'family affair' (Grech 2016). This result also implies that policies aimed to improve household wellbeing need to pay attention to functional difficulties. Indeed, despite the development of social protection programs in recent years in the four countries, deprivations in terms of material wellbeing and food insecurity are widespread, and disproportionately so among households with functional difficulties.

3. For some individual and household outcomes (job type, assets, total expenditures), results were not consistent across countries. In three countries, total expenditures do not differ across functional status, which is consistent with earlier results in the literature. Total expenditures may reflect additional expenditures associated with a functional difficulty (e.g., health, transportation and care expenditures).
4. This analysis also shows that not all persons with functional difficulties are poor; persons with disabilities are not always among the poorest of the poor. Some persons with functional difficulties do achieve levels of wellbeing comparable to persons with no difficulty.
5. The association between functional difficulties and deprivations was found for both severe and moderate functional difficulties, although it was typically larger and more often significant for the former. Moderate functional difficulties are also correlates of deprivations, and there is a severity gradient in the association between deprivations and functional difficulties, consistent with other findings in the literature (Banks et al. 2014).
6. Analyses should try to incorporate the degree of functional difficulties through several categories (e.g., moderate, severe) or a

score. Yet recommendations of the use of the Washington Group questions focus on the group with severe functional difficulties. Analyses that focus on severe functional difficulties leave out persons with moderate functional difficulties who are also at risk of poverty.

7. In addition to functional difficulties, older ages and being female are also correlated with deprivations. This makes older persons with functional difficulties and women with functional difficulties more likely to be multidimensionally poor. These results underscore the importance of considering and addressing age and sex differences when formulating prevention and inclusion strategies with respect to functional status.

Notes

1. There was very limited research conducted prior to 2000 as shown in Elwan (1999). The gray literature has been growing but is included primarily if it pertains to the four countries under study or other countries in Africa.
2. Examples of such qualitative studies include Grech (2015); Eide and Ingstad (2011). For reviews of the literature, see Grech and Soldatic (2016).
3. Eide and Kamaleri (2010) (Lesotho), Eide et al. (2003b) (Namibia), Loeb and Eide (2004) (Malawi), Eide and Kamaleri (2009) (Mozambique), Palmer et al. (2010) (Vietnam), World Bank (2009) (India).
4. Evidence is offered in the following studies, among others: Eide and Mmatli (2016) (Botswana), Loeb and Eide (2004) (Malawi), Gayle-Geddes (2015) (Jamaica), Hoogeveen (2005) (Uganda), Loeb et al. (2008) (South Africa), Mete (2008) (Eastern Europe), Mitra et al. (2013) (15 LMICs), Mont and Cuong (2011) (Vietnam), Rischewski et al. (2008) (Rwanda), Trani and Loeb (2010) (Afghanistan and Zambia), World Bank (2009) (India), WHO-World Bank 2011 (59 countries).
5. Eide and Jele (2011) (Swaziland), Eide and Kamaleri (2010) (Lesotho), Eide and Mmatli (2016) (Botswana), Gayle-Geddes (2015) (Jamaica), Hoogeveen (2005) (Uganda), Mete (2008) and Mussida and Sciulli (2016) (Eastern Europe), Mitra (2008) and NDSD (2015) (South Africa), Mitra and Sambamoorthi (2008) (India), Payne et al. (2013) (Malawi), World Bank (2009) (India), Trani and Loeb (2010) (Afghanistan and Zambia), UNESCAP (2016) (Asia), WHO-World Bank (2011) (59 countries).

6. One can get a sense of the variety of methods under use by reading Filmer (2008), Mitra and Sambamoorthi (2008) and Trani and Loeb (2010).
7. Each variable is weighted using the corresponding eigenvector for the first principal component, found by a principal component analysis.
8. Health expenditures include those associated with inpatient and outpatient contacts, nonprescription medication and medical equipment.
9. Education expenditures are collected at the individual level for all household members who attend school and then aggregated at the household level.
10. Mitra, Palmer et al. (2017) offer a recent review of this literature.
11. A shock is an unexpected negative event. The list of shocks covered in the survey is in Table 5.1.
12. Descriptive statistics are in Table 4.4.
13. Descriptive statistics are in Table 4.7.
14. Results in Sect. 4 on prevalence illustrate this for gender and rural residence.
15. The household functional difficulty score is the highest functional difficulty score among adults aged 15 and above in the household.

References

Adioetomo, M., Mont, D., & Irwanto. (2014). *Persons with disabilities in Indonesia: Empirical facts and implications for social protection policies.* Lembaga Demografi. http://www.tnp2k.go.id/images/uploads/downloads/Disabilities%20report%20Final%20sept2014%20(1).pdf. Accessed 1 March 2017.

Alkire, S., & Foster, J. (2011). Counting and multidimensional poverty measurement. *Journal of Public Economics, 95*, 476–487.

Alkire, S., & Santos, M. E. (2010). *Acute multidimensional poverty: A new index for developing countries.* Oxford: Oxford Poverty and Human Development Initiative.

Alkire, S., & Santos, M. E. (2014). Measuring acute poverty in the developing world: Robustness and scope of the multidimensional poverty index. *World Development, 59*, 251–274.

Baldwin, M. L., & Johnson, W. G. (2005). A critical review of studies of discrimination against workers with disabilities. In W. M. Rodgers III (Ed.), *Handbook on the economics of discrimination* (pp. 119–160). Cheltenham, MD: Edward-Elgar Publishing.

Banks, M. L., & Polack S. (2014). *The economic costs of exclusion and gains of inclusion of people with disabilities: Evidence from low- and middle-income countries.* International Center for Evidence in Disability.

Brucker, D. L., Mitra, S., Chaitoo, N., & Mauro, J. (2015). More likely to be poor whatever the measure: Working age persons with disabilities in the United States. *Social Science Quarterly, 96*(1), 273–296.

Eide, A. H., & Ingstad, B. (Eds.). (2011). *Disability and poverty: A global challenge*. Bristol: Policy Press.

Eide A. H., & Jele, B. (2011). *Living conditions among people with disabilities in Swaziland. A National, Representative Study*. SINTEF A 20047. Oslo: SINTEF Technology & Society.

Eide, A., & Kamaleri, Y. (2009). *Living conditions among people with disabilities in Mozambique. A national representative study*. Oslo: SINTEF Health Research.

Eide, A. H., & Kamaleri, Y. (2010). *Living conditions among people with disability in Lesotho*. Oslo: SINTEF Health Research.

Eide, A. H., & Mmatli, T. (2016). *Living conditions among people with disability in Botswana*. Oslo: SINTEF Health Research.

Eide, A., Nhiwathiwa, S., Muderedzi, J., & Loeb M. (2003a). *Living conditions among people with activity limitations in Zimbabwe. A regional representative survey*. Oslo: SINTEF Health Research.

Eide, A., van Rooy, G., & Loeb, M. (2003b). *Living Conditions among People with Activity Limitations in Namibia. A national representative survey*. Oslo: SINTEF Health Research.

Elwan, A. (1999). *Poverty and disability: A survey of the literature*, (Social protection discussion paper series, No. 9932). Washington, DC: The World Bank.

Filmer, D. (2008). Disability, poverty and schooling in developing countries: Results from 14 household surveys. *The World Bank Economic Review, 22*(1), 141–163.

Filmer, D., & Pritchett, L. H. (2001). Estimating wealth effects without expenditure data—or tears: An application to educational enrollments in states of India. *Demography, 38*(1), 115–132.

Gayle-Geddes, A. (2015). *Disability and inequality: Socioeconomic imperatives and public policy in Jamaica*. London: Palgrave MacMillan.

Grammenos, S. (2013). *European comparative data on Europe 2020 & people with disabilities*. Final report on behalf of the Academic Network of European Disability Experts (ANED).

Grech, S. (2015). *Disability and poverty in the global South. Renegotiating development in Guatemala*. London: Palgrave Macmillan.

Grech, S. (2016). Disability and poverty: Complex interactions and critical reframings. In Grech, S. and Soldatic, K. (eds) (2016). *Disability in the Global South: the Critical Handbook*, pp. 217–236 International Perspectives on Social Policy, Administration and Practice. Switzerland: Springer.

Grech, S., & Soldatic, K. (Eds.). (2016). *Disability in the global south: The critical handbook*. International perspectives on social policy, administration and practice. Cham: Springer.

Groce, N., Kett, M., Lang, R., & Trani, J. F. (2011). Disability and poverty: The need for a more nuanced understanding of implications for development policy and practice. *Third World Quarterly, 32*(8), 1493–1513.

Hoogeveen, J. G. (2005). Measuring welfare for small but vulnerable groups: Poverty and disability in Uganda. *Journal of African Economies, 14*(4), 603–631.

Loeb, M., & Eide, A. (2004). *Living conditions among people with activity limitations in Malawi*. Oslo: SINTEF Health Research.

Loeb, M., Eide, A., Jelsma, J., Toni, M., & Maart, S. (2008). Poverty and disability in eastern and western cape provinces, South Africa. *Disability and Society, 23*(4), 311–321.

Mete, C. (Ed.). (2008). *Economic implications of chronic illness and disability in Eastern Europe and the former Soviet Union*. Washington, DC: World Bank.

Mitra, S. (2008). The recent decline in the employment of persons with disabilities in South Africa, 1998–2006. *South African Journal of Economics, 76*(3), 480–492.

Mitra, S., & Sambamoorthi, U. (2008). Disability and the rural labor market in India: Evidence for males in Tamil Nadu. *World Development, 36*(5), 934–952.

Mitra, S., Posarac, A., & Vick, B. (2013). Disability and poverty in developing countries: A multidimensional study. *World Development, 41*, 1–18.

Mitra, S., Palmer, M., Mont, D., & Groce, N. (2016). Can households cope with health shocks in Vietnam? *Health Economics, 25*(7), 888–907.

Mitra, S., Palmer, M., Kim, H., Mont, D., & Groce, N. (2017). Extra costs of living with a disability: A review and agenda for future research.*Disability and Health*. DOI: http://dx.doi.org/10.1016/j.dhjo.2017.04.007.

Mizunoya, S., & Mitra, S. (2013). Is there a disability gap in employment rates in developing countries? *World Development, 42*, 28–43.

Mizunoya, S., Mitra, S., & Yamasaki, I. (2016). *Towards inclusive education: The impact of disability on school attendance in developing countries*. Innocenti (Working Paper No.2016–03). Florence: UNICEF Office of Research.

Mont, D., & Cuong, N. (2011). Disability and poverty in Vietnam. *World Bank Economic Review, 25*(2), 323–359.

Mussida, C., & Sciulli, D. (2016). Disability and employment across Central and Eastern European countries. *IZA Journal of Labor & Development, 5*, 4.

NDSD. (2015) *Elements of the financial and economic costs of disability to households in South Africa: A pilot study*. Pretoria: National Department of Social Development, Republic of South Africa,.

Palmer, M., Thuy, N., Quyen, Q., Duy, D., Huynh, H., & Berry, H. (2010). Disability measures as an indicator of poverty: A case study from Vietnam. *Journal of International Development*. http://dx.doi.org/10.1002/jid.1715.

Payne, C. F., Mkandawire, J., & Kohler, H.-P. (2013). Disability transitions and health expectancies among adults 45 years and older in Malawi: A cohort-based model. *PLoS Medicine, 10*(5), e1001435. doi:10.1371/journal.pmed.1001435.

Rischewski, D., Kuper, H., Atijosan, O., Simms, V., Jofret-Bonet, M., Foster, A., et al. (2008). Poverty and musculoskeletal impairment in Rwanda. *Transactions of the Royal Society of Tropical Medicine and Hygiene, 102,* 608–617.

She, P., & Livermore, G. (2009). Long-term poverty and disability among working-age adults. *Journal of Disability Policy Studies, 19*(4), 244–256.

Stiglitz, J. E., Sen, A. K., & Fitoussi, J. P. (2009). *Report by the commission on the measurement of economic performance and social progress.* Paris: Commission on the Measurement of Economic Performance and Social Progress. Available at www.stiglitz-sen-fitoussi.fr/en/index.htm.

Trani, J., & Loeb, M. (2010). Poverty and disability: a vicious circle? Evidence from Afghanistan and Zambia.*Journal of International Development, 24*(1), pp. S19–S52.

Trani, J.F., & Canning, T.I.. (2013). Child poverty in an emergency and conflict context: A multidimensional profile andan identification of the poorest children in Western Darfur. *World Development, 48,* 48–70.

Trani, J., Bakhshi, P., Myer Tlapek, S., Lopez, D., & Gall, F. (2015). Disability and poverty in Morocco and Tunisia: A multidimensional approach. *Journal of Human Development and Capabilities, 16*(4), 518–548.

Trani, J., Kuhlberg, J., Cannings, T., & Chakkal, D. (2016). Multidimensional poverty in Afghanistan: Who are the poorest of the poor? *Oxford Development Studies.* doi:10.1080/13600818.2016.1160042.

UNDP. (2016). *Sustainable development goals.* United Nations Development Programme. Available: http://www.undp.org/content/undp/en/home/sustainable-development-goals.html. Accessed August 20, 2016.

UNESCAP. (2016). *Disability at a glance 2015.* Accessed March 3, 2017 http://www.unescap.org/sites/default/files/SDD%20Disability%20Glance%202015_Final.pdf.

WHO–World Bank. (2011). *World report on disability.* Geneva: World Health Organization.

World Bank. (2009). *People with disabilities in India: From commitments to outcomes.* Washington, DC: World Bank.

CHAPTER 6

Dynamics of Functional Difficulties and Wellbeing

Abstract This chapter uses the longitudinal data for Ethiopia, Malawi, Tanzania and Uganda to investigate some dynamic links between disability and wellbeing. The functional difficulty trajectories of individuals are significantly associated with different levels of wellbeing. Persons with persistent functional difficulties are worse off than persons with functional difficulties in one or no period. Women with persistent difficulties and older persons with persistent difficulties are the most deprived groups. New functional difficulties lower the odds to continue working and no longer reporting any difficulty increases the odds of returning to work. Functional difficulties are also associated with mortality in the short-term. More research is needed on the links between disability, on the one hand, and poverty dynamics and mortality, on the other.

Keywords Disability · Panel data · Mortality · Gender · Aging · Africa

JEL I1 · I3 · O15 · J1

In this chapter, I exploit the longitudinal data available for Ethiopia, Malawi, Tanzania, and Uganda to study three questions related to the

S. Mitra, *Disability, Health and Human Development*,
Palgrave Studies in Disability and International Development,
DOI 10.1057/978-1-137-53638-9_6

dynamic links between functional difficulties and wellbeing. The first section asks whether individuals with different trajectories in terms of functional difficulties (e.g., new functional difficulty in wave 2, functional difficulty in both waves) tend to have different characteristics and wellbeing outcomes. The second section investigates if short-term changes in functional difficulties are associated with changes in asset ownership and work status. The last section considers if functional difficulties predict mortality in the short term.

Each of the three sections starts with a literature review, then moves onto methodology and ends with results and discussion. I conclude with a summary of the main results of this chapter. Because the first and second sections require information on functional difficulties in two waves, which was only available in Ethiopia and Uganda, results are limited to these two countries.

6.1 Functional Trajectories and Their Correlates

6.1.1 Literature

Results in Chapter 4 earlier show that transitions in and out of functional difficulties are common. They affect about half of individuals with functional difficulties at a given point in time in Ethiopia and Uganda. This result is consistent with results from studies in HICs. The question then arises as to what such transitions may be correlated with.

There is a small body of literature on these correlates that tries to separate demographic from socioeconomic correlates. It also asks to what extent these transitions are due to factors amenable to policy change (e.g., poverty, employment, and education). The literature is mostly focused on transitions into disability, i.e., on the predictors of onsets. It has consistently shown that older persons are more likely to experience transitions into disability (e.g., Gannon and Nolan 2007). As age may be correlated with educational attainment, studies have to consider the extent to which, within age groups, education predicts onsets. Results are mixed with some studies finding that education predicts onsets (Jenkins and Rigg 2003; Jagger et al. 2007; Burchardt 2003) and other studies finding that it does not (Gannon and Nolan 2007). There is also evidence that poverty is a significant predictor of later disability onset while gender and family composition are not (Burchardt 2003; Gannon and Nolan 2007; Jenkins and Rigg 2003).

The literature on the determinants of persistent difficulties and of transitions out of disability is even smaller. Gannon and Nolan (2007) find that persons who are older, male and unemployed, and have no education are more likely to have a persistent illness or disability. They also find that people who work are more likely to no longer report an illness or disability in a subsequent wave compared to people who do not work. Jagger et al. (2007) show that persons with limited educational attainment are less likely to experience a transition out of a mobility or ADL limitation.

The literature above uses several disability measures: a broad activity limitation or work limitation measure (Burchardt 2003; Jenkins and Rigg 2003), a mobility or ADL limitation (e.g., Jagger et al. 2007) or broadly, a health problem, illness, or disability (Gannon and Nolan 2007). The question then arises as to whether similar correlates can also be found when one uses the Washington Group short set of questions on disability, which are now increasingly used in surveys and censuses internationally, but largely in cross-sectional datasets. The literature above is set in the context of a few HICs (Ireland, UK, and USA). Do similar results hold in very different contexts, in LICs in particular where healthcare and rehabilitation services, and the socioeconomic environment are very different? This is what the rest of this section attempts to answer for Ethiopia and Uganda.

6.1.2 Methodology

The objective of this section is to determine the correlates of different trajectories in functional difficulty status in the short term. If persons with persistent functional difficulties are found to have a different profile compared to persons with transitory or no difficulty, it will be important to monitor this group for policy and to understand the determinants and consequences of persistent difficulties.

This section is focused on the cases of Ethiopia and Uganda, where comparable data on functional difficulties using the Washington Group questions was collected in two waves: the Ethiopia Rural Socioeconomic Survey (2011/2012, 2013/2014) and the Uganda National Panel Survey (2009/2010, 2010/2011). The sample includes individuals whose functional status is known in both waves.[1]

Individuals are categorized into one of four functional difficulty categories depending on their trajectory: (1) A functional difficulty in wave 1 only; (2) A functional difficulty in wave 2 only; (3) A functional difficulty in both waves; and (4) No functional difficulty in any wave. The analysis not only considers any degree of functional difficulty (moderate or severe), but also later separates transitions by degree (severe, then moderate). Given that the longitudinal data is available for the short term only, the permanent or temporary nature of a functional difficulty cannot be determined. (1) and (2) may get at exits or entries into a functional difficulty status, but may also capture episodic functional difficulties. Group (1) captures persons with medium, long-term, or permanent functional difficulties. As noted in Chapter 4, there could be a variety of reasons for reporting a functional difficulty in one wave and not in the other, including changes in reporting behavior, measurement error, and actual changes in functional limitations.

After presenting descriptive statistics, this section will give results of a multinomial logit model of the probability of experiencing a particular functional trajectory as presented in Box 4.

Box 4: Multinomial logit model of functional trajectories

$$\textit{Functional Trajectory}_{i,t+1} = \alpha + \beta\, \textit{Deprivation}_{i,t} + \sum_k \gamma_k x_{i,k,t} + \varepsilon_{i,t} \qquad (6.1)$$

where:

- $\textit{Functional Trajectory}_{i,t+1}$ of individual i at time $t+1$ refers to the four categories of functional trajectory above (1) through (4) with (4) No functional difficulty in any wave as the reference category.
- α is the intercept;
- $\textit{Deprivation}_{i,t}$ is a dummy variable equal to 1 if the individual experiences a deprivation in the previous wave (in turn with respect to education, morbidity, work, material wellbeing, economic insecurity, and multidimensional poverty), 0 otherwise;
- β is the coefficient of the deprivation status to be estimated. Results are reported in Table 6.2.
- $x_{i,k,t}$ is a set of k control variables at the individual, household or community level in time t (age categories, male, married, household head, household size, rural residence, distance to healthcare services);
- γ_k is the set of estimated coefficients of the k control variables;
- $\varepsilon_{i,t}$ is the error term for person i at time t.

Model (6.1) of Box 4 does not identify the causal link from recent characteristics or deprivations to recent changes in functional difficulty. Instead, it estimates an association. For instance, finding a positive and significant coefficient for material wellbeing deprivation in wave 1 for a new functional status in wave 2 does not indicate that the material deprivation in wave 1 caused the functional difficulty in wave 2. It might reflect reverse causality from functional difficulty to a deprivation: the functional difficulty may have been a long term but transitory functional difficulty that was not measured in wave 1 and yet had already affected the employment, earnings, and material wellbeing of the individual prior to wave 1. The material wellbeing deprivation and the functional difficulty may also both be caused by factors not measured in the model, such as violence, natural disasters or an absence of public goods in the community (e.g., infrastructure, health services).

6.1.2.1 Results and Discussion

Table 6.1 gives descriptive statistics for four groups of individuals based on their functional difficulty trajectory. Consistent with the descriptive statistics with cross-sectional data earlier in Chapter 4 (Table 4.4), persons with no functional difficulty tend to be younger and belong to larger households. In Ethiopia, males and females are evenly spread across the four groups, while in Uganda, 61% of persons with persistent functional limitations are women. There is no significant difference in the distance to healthcare services across groups, except in Uganda where persons with persistent difficulties are further away on average.

Table 6.1 also shows that the functional trajectory is associated with patterns with respect to deprivations in five dimensions (education, morbidity, work, material wellbeing, and insecurity) and in the multidimensional poverty indicators of Chapter 5 (H, A, M_0). Persons with persistent functional difficulties are worse off than persons with functional difficulties in wave 1 or 2 and persons with no functional limitation in any wave. This is shown by significantly higher rates of deprivation in each dimension and of multidimensional poverty. For instance, in Ethiopia, 87% of those with persistent difficulties are multidimensionally poor compared to 69% of those who do not experience any difficulty in waves 1 and 2, and, respectively, 85 and 74% of those with a difficulty in wave 1 or 2 only.

Results from the model in Box 4 are shown in Table 6.2 for transitions in severe functional difficulty in the top panel, moderate difficulties in the middle panel, and then for all difficulties (any degree) in the bottom

Table 6.1 Descriptive statistics by functional difficulty trajectory

	Ethiopia				*Uganda*			
	Difficulty in wave 1 only	*Difficulty in wave 2 only*	*Persistent diff. in both waves*	*No difficulty*	*Difficulty in wave 1 only*	*Difficulty in wave 2 only*	*Persistent diff. in both waves*	*No difficulty*
Personal factors								
Age 15–39	0.39***	0.35***	0.18***	0.72	0.4***	0.35***	0.22***	0.76
Age 40–49	0.18***	0.19***	0.19***	0.15	0.19***	0.23***	0.12***	0.13
Age 50–64	0.29***	0.28***	0.24***	0.09	0.27***	0.27***	0.27***	0.08
Age 65+	0.15***	0.18***	0.39***	0.03	0.14***	0.15***	0.39***	0.02
Male	0.47	0.49	0.5*	0.5	0.47**	0.48	0.39***	0.5
Structural factors								
Household								
Married	0.74**	0.69	0.63***	0.69	0.55**	0.54***	0.49	0.52
Household head	0.57***	0.6***	0.65	0.38	0.57***	0.58	0.62	0.33
Household size	5.44***	5.35***	4.5***	5.8	6.95***	7.31***	6.47***	7.5
	(0.12)	(0.14)	(0.15)	(0.04)	(0.23)	(0.52)	(0.27)	(0.07)
Community								
Distance to healthcare services	15.41	16.5	14.41	15.4	28.38	26.45	28.06**	26.37
	(0.77)	(0.96)	(0.83)	(0.26)	(1.91)	(2.23)	(1.94)	(0.72)
Rural	NA	NA	NA	NA	0.85***	0.89**	0.88***	0.84
Deprivations								
Education	0.93***	0.93***	0.97***	0.81	0.64***	0.55***	0.73***	0.4
Morbidity	0.4***	0.24***	0.48***	0.18	0.46***	0.55***	0.62***	0.29
Employment	0.25	0.23	0.33***	0.24	0.21*	0.24	0.36***	0.25
Material	0.99**	0.99	0.99**	0.98	0.71***	0.7***	0.71***	0.66
Insecurity	0.39***	0.3	0.37***	0.34	0.59***	0.6***	0.62***	0.48
H	0.85***	0.74	0.87***	0.69	0.71***	0.72***	0.79***	0.49
A	0.6***	0.57***	0.63***	0.56	0.54***	0.55***	0.61***	0.5
	(0.01)	(0.01)	(0.01)	(0.00)	(0.01)	(0.01)	(0.01)	(0.00)
M_0	0.52***	0.42**	0.55**	0.38	0.38***	0.4***	0.48***	0.24
	(0.01)	(0.02)	(0.02)	(0.00)	(0.01)	(0.03)	(0.02)***	(0.00)
N	*611*	*485*	*457*	*6360*	*504*	*401*	*558*	*4527*

Notes The characteristics and deprivations are for wave 1. *** significant at the 1% level, ** significant at the 5% level, *significant at the 10% level.

Table 6.2 Odds ratio of deprivation by functional trajectory

	Ethiopia			*Uganda*		
	Difficulty in wave 1 only	*Difficulty in wave 2 only*	*Persistent difficulty in both waves*	*Difficulty in wave 1 only*	*Difficulty in wave 2 only*	*Persistent difficulty in both waves*
Severe difficulty transitions						
Education	1.21	3.94**	3.98***	2.57***	1.79	3.56***
Morbidity	4.02***	1.2	5.47***	1.23	7.1***	3.76***
Employment	2.18***	1.65*	3.76***	1.03	2.54**	5.61***
Material wellbeing	3.25*	1.7	4.32**	1.19	0.81	1.45
Insecurity	1.87**	0.45**	2.47***	2.15***	3.1***	1.38
Multidimensional poverty	2.27***	0.99	5.1***	2.31***	4.98***	4.75***
Moderate difficulty transitions						
Education	1.44**	1.01	1.93**	1.34**	1.17	1.19
Morbidity	2.5***	1.17	2.24***	1.53***	2.41***	2.51***
Employment	1	1.03	1.02	1.07	1.06	1.07
Material wellbeing	1.72*	0.8	0.87	1.29*	1.08	0.92
Insecurity	1.55	0.85	0.99	1.39***	1.68***	1.86***
Multidimensional poverty	1.95***	0.91	1.82***	1.63***	2.01***	1.96***
All transitions						
Education	1.41**	1.16	2.62***	1.48***	1.24	1.75***
Morbidity	2.7***	1.17	2.94***	1.45***	2.56***	3.01***
Employment	1.14	1.08	1.54***	1.05	1.15	2.02***
Material wellbeing	1.97***	0.61*	1.24	1.3**	1.06	1.11
Insecurity	1.79***	0.72**	1.51***	1.42***	1.73***	1.97***
Multidimensional poverty	1.99***	0.92 NS	2.49***	1.7***	2.16***	2.92***

Notes For each deprivation in a given row, a multinomial logit regression as in Box 4 is run and the odds ratio of difficulty in wave 1 only, difficulty in wave 2 only and difficulty in both waves are reported on the same row. No functional difficulty in any wave is the reference category. The upper (middle) panel covers severe (moderate) difficulty transitions and excludes persons with a moderate (severe) difficulty in any wave. ***significant at the 1% level, **significant at the 5% level, *significant at the 10% level. More information on the dependent variables is in Table 5.2. Descriptive statistics are in Table 6.1

panel. Persons with persistent functional difficulties are significantly more likely to have experienced multidimensional poverty and a deprivation in any dimension in Ethiopia and most dimensions in Uganda compared to persons with no functional difficulty in any wave. A similar association is found for persons with a severe limitation in wave 1 or wave 2, albeit less strong. Comparing the results of severe and moderate functional difficulty transitions, overall similar results are found for moderate difficulties but with smaller odds ratios.

Next, the mean adjusted multidimensional poverty headcount (M_0)[2] is calculated for different groups of persons with functional difficulties based on age, sex, and the severity and trajectory of the functional difficulty.[3] The trajectory covers a functional difficulty in one wave vs. both waves. Results are presented in Fig. 6.1. Groups are ranked from the least (bottom) to the most (top) multidimensionally poor as measured by M_0. There is a considerable variation in M_0 across the subgroups ranging 0.45–0.7 in Ethiopia and 0.3–0.6 in Uganda.

There are some patterns in both countries. Older persons, older women, and persons experiencing severe difficulties in both waves tend to be the groups the most multidimensionally poor. These are groups for whom personal factors, structural factors, resources, and functional difficulties may interact to create situations of extreme deprivations. Further research is needed that explores the heterogeneity in wellbeing of persons with functional difficulties and how they are shaped by personal, structural, and resource factors.

6.2 Changes in Functional Difficulties and Economic Wellbeing

6.2.1 *Literature Review*

As noted in Chapter 2, it is often stated that 'disability and poverty are a cause and a consequence of each other' (DFID 2000; Yeo and Moore 2003). Yet, the poverty dynamics literature has been largely silent on disability. From the poverty dynamics literature, we know that households in LMICs have a limited set of coping mechanisms to deal with the economic consequences of illness, hospitalization or broad activity limitations (Santos et al. 2011; Mitra et al. 2016). In fact, they sometimes adopt coping mechanisms that are detrimental in the medium and long

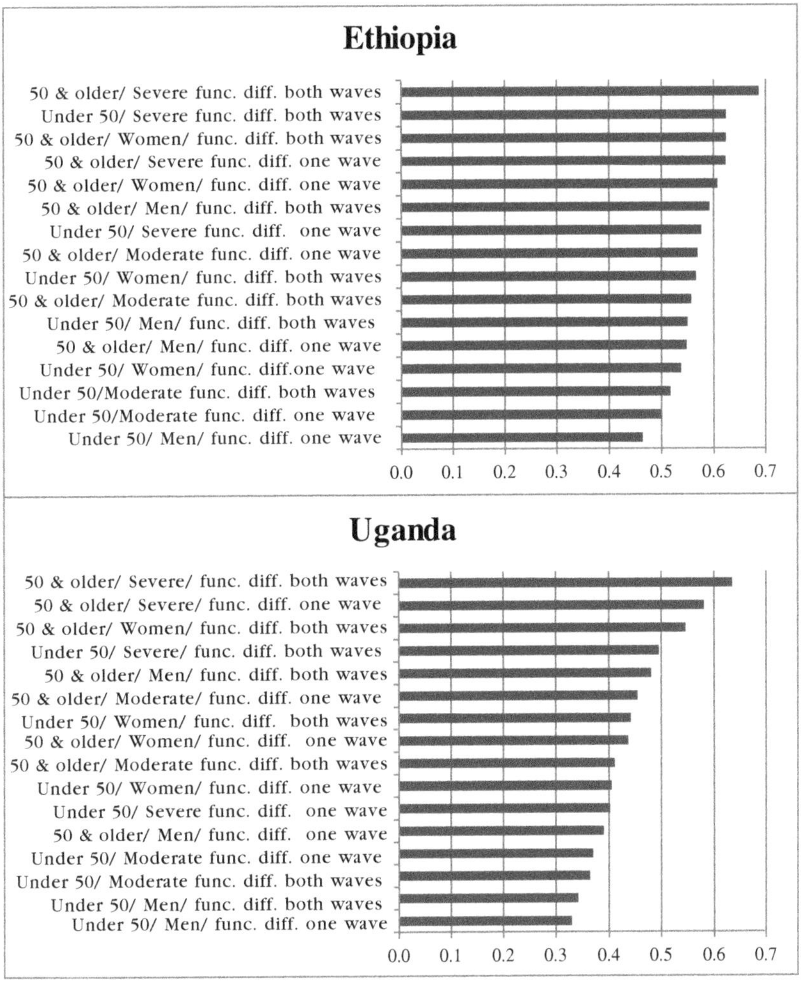

Fig. 6.1 Multidimensional poverty adjusted headcount (M_0) by subgroup

run, such as selling productive assets. WHO–World Bank (2011) notes that the onset of disability is linked with a decline in social and economic wellbeing and an increase in poverty through a number of channels including stigma, education, employment, inaccessible basic services, and increased disability-related expenditures. However, the evidence for these complex relationships between disability and deprivations is very limited. The evidence is scarce (Grech 2015) and is mainly correlational and does not separate the many causal pathways between disability and wellbeing (Groce et al. 2011; Mitra et al. 2013; Minuzoya and Mitra 2013).

The causal literature is mainly on the pathways from poverty to disability through channels such as malnutrition and working conditions. This suggests that policies aiming at poverty reduction in general will reduce disability prevalence. Poverty, and more broadly, inequalities, may increase the risk of disability through several pathways, many of which are related to poor health and its determinants. Poverty may lead to the onset of a health condition that results in disability. In LMICs, there is evidence that malnutrition leads to disability (Maulik and Damstadt 2007). Other possible pathways include diseases whose incidence and prevalence are strongly associated with poverty, lack of inadequate public health interventions (e.g., immunization), poor living conditions (e.g., lack of safe water), environmental exposures (e.g., unsafe work environments), and injuries. Poverty, as a contextual factor, may also increase the likelihood that a health condition/impairment/functional difficulty may result in a disability, for instance, if there is a lack of healthcare and rehabilitation services or if there are barriers to access the services that are available. In addition, stigma associated with a health condition or impairment may lead to deprivations. It might also be worsened by the stigma associated with poverty. Limited resources in the community, for instance to build accessible roads or buildings, may also make it difficult for an individual with mobility impairment to participate in the community life.

In reverse, the onset of a disability may lead to lower living standards and poverty through adverse impacts on education, employment, earnings, and increased expenditures related to disability. Disability may prevent school attendance for children and youth with disabilities (Filmer 2008; Mizunoya et al. 2016) and restrict their human capital accumulation, thus leading to limited employment opportunities and reduced productivity (earnings) in adulthood. For onsets during adulthood, disability may prevent work, or constrain the kind and amount of work a person can do (Gertler and Gruber 2002), lowering income for the individual and the household and potentially resulting in poverty. In addition, disability may lead to additional expenditures for the individual and the household, in particular in relation to specific services such as healthcare, transportation, assistive devices, personal care (Mont and Cuong 2011; Mitra et al. 2017).

6.2.2 Methodology

6.2.2.1 Household Material Wellbeing

I exploit the longitudinal data available for Ethiopia and Uganda to investigate if changes in functional difficulties are associated with changes in economic wellbeing between two waves two years apart for Ethiopia and one year apart for Uganda. For the asset index, a first-difference model is estimated where changes in asset score between two waves are associated with changes in control variables at the household level (Table 4.7). Based on the human development model (Chapter 2) and the associations between economic deprivations and functional difficulties found in Chapter 5, a functional difficulty decrease/increase is expected to be associated with an increase/decrease in economic wellbeing, respectively.

For work status, the model is described in Box 5. I split the analysis between individuals who are working at baseline and those who are not and differentiate between increasing and decreasing functional difficulties. The objective is to investigate separately determinants of work exits, on the one hand, and return to work, on the other (Mitra and Jones 2017). Among persons working at wave 1, I also restrict the sample to persons without a functional difficulty at baseline. I then investigate if an increase in functional difficulty is associated with an increase in the probability of transitioning into not working. Likewise, among persons not working at wave 1, I investigate the decrease in functional difficulty and its association with returning to work for the sample of the initially not working with a functional difficulty in wave 1.

Box 5: First-difference model of work status

$$\Delta y_i = \beta \; \Delta F_i + \sum_{k=1}^{5} \gamma_k \Delta x_{k,i} + \Delta \varepsilon_i \tag{6.2}$$

where:

- The symbol Δ refers to the difference of a given variable between wave *t+1* and *t*;
- Δy_i denotes changes in work status for individual *i*: work exit and return to work transitions are considered in turn as dependent variable.
- ΔF_i is the change in functional difficulties: for work exit, the sample includes persons with no difficulty and working in wave 1 and a value of '1' refers to a new difficulty in wave 2, a value of

'0' refers to no change; for return to work, the sample includes persons with a difficulty and not working in wave 1, a value of '1' refers to no longer having a difficulty in wave 2, and '0' refers to still having a difficulty in wave 2.
- β is the estimated coefficient for ΔF_i and is reported in Table 6.3.
- The set of control variables includes k potentially time-varying characteristics $\Delta x_{k,i}$ (marital status, household head, household size, distance to healthcare services, rural) while time-invariant characteristics (e.g., sex, birth year) are differenced out.
- γ_k is the set of estimated coefficients of the k control variables.
- $\Delta \varepsilon_i$ captures changes in time-varying unobserved factors.

6.2.3 *Results and Discussion*

6.2.3.1 Household Material Wellbeing

Are changes in functional status associated with changes in household material wellbeing in the short-term? It might be that following an onset of a functional difficulty, households sell assets to pay for healthcare or compensate for lower earnings.

In the interest of space, results of the asset index are discussed here but are not shown in a table. Changes in functional difficulties are not significantly associated with changes in asset ownership for Ethiopia and Uganda.

The differences in asset ownership shown earlier in Chapter 5 (Table 5.7) for Ethiopia may reflect cumulative effects that take place over the medium and long term and could not be identified here with data following households over the short term. They may also reflect other links between functional difficulties and assets/living conditions, including of course reverse causality from poor assets/living conditions to the onset of functional difficulties or other factors that affect both assets/living conditions and functional difficulties.

6.2.3.2 Work Status

Results are presented in Table 6.3 for changes in work status and functional difficulties. Column (i) considers if new functional difficulties in wave 2 are associated with work exits among workers in wave 1. The model gives a significant association between increased functional

Table 6.3 Odds ratio of work exit or return to work and change in functional difficulties

Dependent variable *Functional difficulty transition*	*Work exit* *Difficulty in wave 2 only vs. No difficulty in any wave* *(i)*	*Return to work* *Difficulty in wave 1 only vs. Difficulty in both waves* *(ii)*
Severe difficulty		
Ethiopia		
All	1.72**	4.61***
Females	1.37	3.60*
Males	2.19***	7.92**
Age 15–49	1.11	4.90*
Age 50 and older	2.14***	4.69**
Uganda		
All	2.04**	3.47***
Females	2.11**	2.32
Males	1.63	6.10**
Age 15–49	0.86	3.31
Age 50 and older	3.08***	4.08**
Any difficulty (moderate and severe)		
Ethiopia		
All	1.13	2.99***
Females	1.14	2.39***
Males	1.11	5.40***
Age 15–49	0.86	1.78
Age 50 and older	1.44**	3.66***
Uganda		
All	0.77	2.67***
Females	0.63	2.38**
Males	0.94	3.32**
Age 15–49	0.56*	2.16*
Age 50 and older	1.25	2.37*

Notes Diff. stands for difficulty. Each estimated coefficient is from a separate logistic regression as explained in Box 5. In column (i), the sample includes all individuals working in wave 1 and not reporting a functional difficulty in wave 1. In column (i), a difficulty in wave 2 only refers to: in the upper panel, among persons with no severe difficulty in wave 1, a new severe difficulty in wave 2; and in the lower panel, among persons with no difficulty in wave 1, a new moderate or severe difficulty in wave 2. In column (ii), the sample includes all individuals not working in wave 1 and reporting a functional difficulty in wave 1: no longer experiencing a severe difficulty in the upper panel and no longer experiencing any difficulty at all in the lower panel. ***significant at the 1% level, **significant at the 5% level, *significant at the 10% level

difficulty and rising odds of a work exit when individuals experience new severe difficulties in wave 2 (top panel). This result holds for the entire sample of workers and for older workers in both countries. For instance, for Ethiopia, having a new severe functional difficulty is associated with having 1.7 times higher odds of leaving work.

In contrast, for both countries, when all new functional difficulties, whether moderate or severe, are considered (bottom panel), no significant association is found for the entire sample and all subsamples except persons 50 and older in Ethiopia and persons 15–49 in Uganda.

Column (ii) assesses if changes in functional difficulties are associated with return to work among persons who did not work and had functional difficulties in wave 1. In both countries, no longer experiencing a functional difficulty in wave 2, whether of any degree or severe only, is significantly associated with higher odds of working in wave 2. For Uganda, persons who no longer experience a functional difficulty have odds of working in wave 2 that are 2.7 times higher than persons who still have a functional difficulty.

Does this model identify the causal impact of functional difficulties on work? Compared to the regression models used in Chapter 5 (Table 5.4), the model of Box 5 removes the potential bias of omitted variables associated with time-invariant characteristics (e.g., personality traits such as low self-esteem) that may be correlated with both economic outcomes on the one hand, and reports of functional difficulties, on the other. However, there is still the possibility that these estimates are biased by other factors that change over time, affect both functional difficulties and work status and are not measured here (e.g., exposure to violence). In addition, in each wave, the data on functional difficulties and work were collected at the same time. In other words, in column (i), the new functional difficulty and work exits are observed at the same time in wave 2, and there is no indication of which one preceded the other. Hence, although it is plausible that this temporal association reflects a mechanism whereby functional difficulties impact work status, these results cannot for certain establish a causal link from functional difficulties to work status. More econometric research and qualitative research are needed to isolate and demonstrate the causal links between functional difficulties and work in the context of LICs. Longitudinal datasets that follow individuals over longer periods of time and for more than two waves would help further research in this field.

Nonetheless, these results offer suggestive evidence that functional difficulties may have a negative economic impact through work. New functional difficulties are associated with lower odds of work and no longer reporting difficulties comes with higher odds of return to work in the short term. These findings have implications for public policy. There may be a need for rehabilitation services in an LMIC context to assist people continue working or return to work following the onset of a health deprivation. The availability of vocational rehabilitation services in an LMIC context is limited (WHO–World Bank 2011). In some LMICs, there are programs focused on those injured in the workplace (e.g., Malaysia). In more and more LMICs, there are community-based rehabilitation programs, the efficacy of which is often not evaluated (WHO–World Bank 2011; Mitra et al. 2014). Exceptions are some studies reviewed by Sharma (2007) and recently Mauro et al. (2014, 2015).

6.3 Functional Difficulties and Mortality Within 2 Years

LICs have the highest adult mortality rates in the world (Rajaratnam et al. 2010), and reducing premature adult mortality rates is fundamental to improve wellbeing and to promote sustainable development. Yet data on adult mortality is severely lacking in LICs, as they often do not have vital registry systems. Population-based surveys can offer a way of assessing the overall health of a population (e.g., Rathod et al. 2016).

The objective of this section is to use longitudinal population-level data on mortality collected as part of the LSMS in Ethiopia, Malawi, Tanzania, and Uganda to investigate the association between functional difficulty, on the one hand, and short term mortality, on the other. If important associations are found, then functional difficulty indicators may be considered as potential indicators of vulnerability to mortality for policy purposes.

6.3.1 Methodology

Mortality data was collected as part of the four longitudinal LSMS surveys described in Chapter 3. During a household revisit, the household respondent was asked about each member of the household who was listed as member of the household during the prior wave. In case a member is no longer a part of the household, the household respondent was asked why the person is no longer a member and death is one of the possible reasons listed in the questionnaire. While this survey-based data may provide useful insights, it is limited in that the death cannot be verified and the cause and timing of death are also not known. Certain stigmatized causes of death such as HIV/AIDS may lead to death under-reporting. In the four countries under study, and especially in Malawi, it is likely that HIV/AIDS is a significant cause of death. This section uses a lagged model that exploits the longitudinal data as shown in Box 6.

Box 6: Lagged logistic model of mortality

A logistic regression is run as follows:

$$Mortality_{i,t+1} = \alpha + \beta_1 Severe_{i,t} + \beta_2 Moderate_{i,t} + \sum_k \gamma_k x_{i,t,k} + \delta z_{i,j,t} + \varepsilon_{i,t} \qquad (6.3)$$

where

- $Mortality_{i,t+1}$ is a variable indicating if individual i interviewed in initial wave t died by wave $t+1$ two years later (1 if dead, 0 otherwise).
- α is the intercept;
- $Severe_{i,t}$ is a variable equal to 1 if the individual i had a severe functional difficulty in the initial wave t, 0 otherwise;
- $Moderate_{i,t}$ is a dummy variable equal to 1 if the individual i had a moderate functional difficulty in initial wave t, 0 otherwise;
- β_1 and β_2 are the coefficient of the functional difficulty variables, to be estimated;
  They are the coefficients of interest, and their values are reported for each country in Table 6.5.
- $x_{i,t,k}$ is a set of k control variables for personal factors (age categories, male) and structural factors (being married, being the household head, having a mother with no prior schooling, household size, distance to healthcare services.[4])
- γ_k are the estimated coefficients for the set of k control variables.
- $z_{i,j,t}$ is a binary variable indicating if the person's household is in the bottom quintile based on the asset index described in Chapter 5.
- δ is the estimated coefficient for $z_{i,j,t}$.
- $\varepsilon_{i,t}$ is the error term for person i.

In a variant of (6.3), the functional difficulty variables are replaced by the functional score defined earlier in Chapter 3. Results are also reported in Table 6.5.

6.3.2 Results and Discussion

Adult mortality rates are presented in Table 6.4. They range from a low of 12.4/1000 persons in Uganda to a high of 29/1000 persons in Malawi. In all four countries, men have higher mortality rates than women. Mortality rates are consistent with rates found from other population-based surveys in LICs in Africa.[5] Malawi's mortality rates stand at more than twice those of Ethiopia, Tanzania, and Uganda, which may be due in part of the higher prevalence of HIV/AIDS in Malawi.

Descriptive statistics for the entire sample and the subsamples of persons who died are in Appendix A8. Entire samples have a mean age of about 34 years and mostly include rural residents. As expected, compared with the entire sample, persons who have died were older, more likely to report a functional difficulty and to have fewer assets in the prior wave.

Table 6.5 reports results of the model of Box 6. It gives the odds of dying in the short run, given a functional difficulty (or a functional score value) in the prior wave. Results are given separately by sex and age group. Severe functional difficulties and the functional score are significantly and positively associated with short-term mortality in all four countries for men and women, for people younger or older than 50. For example, in Tanzania,

Table 6.4 Rates of mortality within two years among adults (deaths/1000)

	Ethiopia	*Malawi*	*Tanzania*	*Uganda*
All adults	13.4	29	12.7	12.4
Men	16.2	31.3	15.5	14.7
Women	10.6	26.7	10.2	10.2
Adults younger than 50	7.4	17.1	8	6
Adults 50 and older	40.3	85.4	32.7	43.1

Sources Author's calculations using Ethiopia Rural Socioeconomic Survey (2011/2012, 2013/2014), Malawi Integrated Household Survey (2010/2011, 2012/2013), Tanzania National Panel Survey (2010/2011, 2012/2013) and Uganda National Panel Survey (2009/2010, 2011). *Note* Estimates are weighted

Table 6.5 Odds ratio of short term death by functional difficulty status

	Ethiopia	*Malawi*	*Tanzania*	*Uganda*
Men				
Moderate functional difficulty	2.53***	2.13***	1.82*	1.71
Severe functional difficulty	13.86***	8.98***	6.18***	9.23***
Functional difficulty score	8.07***	10.37***	6.81***	7.69***
Women				
Moderate functional difficulty	2.84**	2.55***	2.52**	7.62***
Severe functional difficulty	10.79***	2.99**	9.99***	26.44***
Functional difficulty score	7.97***	5.37***	7.89***	8.70***
Younger than 50				
Moderate functional difficulty	2.49**	1.21	3.13***	2.55**
Severe functional difficulty	9.90***	6.79***	7.26***	8.75***
Functional difficulty score	9.59***	7.67***	10.12***	6.65***
50 and older				
Moderate functional difficulty	1.39	1.45	1.01	1.39
Severe functional difficulty	7.05**	2.28**	4.28***	5.64***
Functional difficulty score	5.99**	3.46***	5.36***	5.75***

Sources Author's calculations using Ethiopia Rural Socioeconomic Survey (2011/2012, 2013/2014), Malawi Integrated Household Survey (2010/2011, 2012/2013), Tanzania National Panel Survey (2010/2011, 2012/2013) and Uganda National Panel Survey (2009/2010, 2011). *Notes* For each country, two logistic regressions are run. For the first one, the coefficients of moderate difficulty and severe difficulty dummies are reported on separate rows (no functional difficulty is the reference category). For the second one, the coefficient of the functional difficulty score (marginal effect) is reported. Coefficients are odds ratios. ***significant at the 1% level, **significant at the 5% level, *significant at the 10% level. The regression controls are as follows: age, sex (for the sub sample by age), being married, having a mother with no prior schooling, household asset bottom quintile, being the household head, household size, distance to healthcare services and rural. For Tanzania, data was missing for distance to healthcare services for a sizeable share of the sample, community fixed effects were thus used instead

the odds ratios of dying within two years for a woman with a severe functional difficulty are 9.99 times those of a woman with no functional difficulty, everything else held constant. For moderate functional difficulties, an association is found for women in the four countries and for people younger than 50 in three out of four countries. Across all countries and subgroups, a 1% increase in the functional score increases the odds of dying by 5 to 10%.

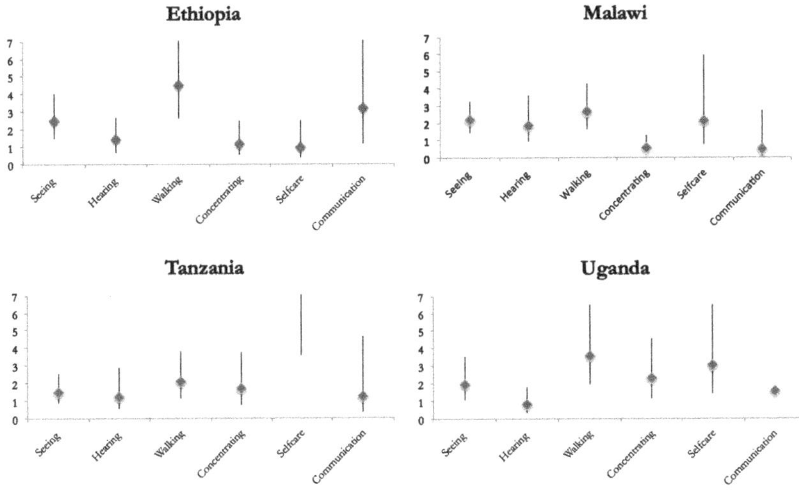

Fig. 6.2 Odds ratio of death within two years by functional difficulty type (any degree) in wave 1.
Note: The estimated odds ratio for selfcare in Tanzania stands at 7.74 and is not shown in the graph

This model is also used by replacing the severe and moderate functional difficulty variables with the type of functional difficulty the person experienced in the initial wave. Results are presented in Fig. 6.2. It plots the odds ratios of death within two years given functional difficulty types (e.g., seeing) in the initial wave and their confidence intervals. A lower bound of the confidence interval above one indicates significantly higher odds of experiencing death within two years compared to a person without this functional difficulty type, everything else held constant. Only one type of functional difficulty, walking, is consistently and significantly associated with higher odds of death in all countries. Having a seeing difficulty is associated with higher odds of death in three countries (Ethiopia, Malawi, and Uganda). There is an association for Selfcare in two countries (Tanzania and Uganda), for communication in Ethiopia and concentrating in Uganda, and none for hearing. Similar results were reached when the analysis was restricted to severe functional difficulties (Appendix A9).[6]

Of course, this model is unable to determine a causal relationship from functional difficulties to mortality. It only points at an association.

Despite this caveat, the results have noteworthy implications. The association between functional difficulties and mortality in the short term has implications for research on disability and poverty. The association between disability and economic inequalities measured at a given point in time as done earlier in Chapter 5 may be affected by a disproportionate risk of mortality associated with disability in the context of LICs. It is therefore possible that due to mortality, the association between disability and poverty using survey data at one point in time may underestimate the true extent of the association between disability and poverty given the disproportionate risk of mortality among the poor with disabilities. Further research is needed on the links between disability, poverty, and mortality.

More broadly, persons with functional difficulties experience higher odds of mortality in the short term. This should be taken into account in policies and programs aimed at reducing mortality among adults, including premature mortality. Functional difficulties may be part of, or linked to, determinants of premature mortality, and yet they are not part of initiatives such as the 25 × 25 initiative signed by WHO members states in 2011 to cut mortality due to noncommunicable diseases by 25% by 2025 (WHO 2013).

6.4 Conclusion: Summary and Implications

This chapter uses longitudinal data for Ethiopia, Malawi, Tanzania, and Uganda to assess some potential dynamic links between functional difficulties and wellbeing.

1. The functional difficulty trajectories of individuals are significantly associated with different levels of wellbeing. Persons with persistent functional difficulties are worse off than persons with functional difficulties in only one wave, who are in turn worse off than persons with no functional limitation in any wave.
2. Among persons with functional difficulties, older persons, older women and persons experiencing persistent severe difficulties tend to be the groups the most multidimensionally poor.

   Longitudinal data collection and monitoring of functional difficulties and wellbeing outcomes are needed to identify the trajectory of functional difficulties and vulnerable groups. This is required for policies and programs that aim to reduce extreme poverty in general and to target vulnerable groups in particular.

3. No significant association was found between changes in functional status and changes in assets/living conditions in the short term.
4. New functional difficulties lower the odds to continue working, and no longer reporting functional difficulties increases the odds of returning to work.

   These findings suggest that there may be a causal link from functional difficulties to work status.

   These findings, together with the consistent and strong association between functional difficulties and work outcomes found in Chapter 5, suggest that there may be a need for rehabilitation services in an LMIC context to assist people to continue working or return to work following the onset of a health deprivation.
5. Functional difficulties are consistently found to be associated with mortality in the short term.

   More attention is needed to functional difficulties as potential determinants of mortality, including premature mortality. More research is also needed on the links between disability, poverty, and mortality as excess mortality may reduce the association between disability and poverty in LICs.

Notes

1. Attrition was very limited for both datasets.
2. M_0 is explained earlier in Chapter 5.
3. Groups could not be further disaggregated due to small sample sizes: for instance, the sample could not be disaggregated by age, sex, trajectory *and* severity.
4. Descriptive statistics are in Table 4.4.
5. For instance, for Zambia, Rathod et al. (2016) find a mortality rate of 16.2/1000 for men and 12.3/1000 for women.
6. Given the association between functional difficulties and resources, especially asset ownership, the model is also run without economic quintile as a control. Results were overall similar for the functional difficulty/score variables.

References

Burchardt, T. (2003). *Being and becoming: Social exclusion and the onset of disability* (ESRC Centre for Analysis of Social Exclusion (CASE) Report 21).

DFID. (2000). *Disability, poverty and development* (Issues Paper). London: Department for International Development. http://hpod.org/pdf/Disability-poverty-and-development.pdf. Accessed 13 Jan 2017.

Filmer, D. (2008). Disability, poverty and schooling in developing countries: Results from 14 household surveys. *The World Bank Economic Review, 22*(1), 141–163.

Gannon, B., & Nolan, B. (2007). Transitions in disability and work. *Estudios de Economía Aplicada, 25*(2), 447–472.

Gertler, P., & Gruber, J. (2002). Insuring consumption against illness. *American Economic Review, 92*(1), 51–70.

Grech, S. (2015). *Disability and poverty in the global south. Renegotiating development in Guatemala.* London: Palgrave Macmillan.

Groce, N., Kett, M., Lang, R., & Trani, J. F. (2011). Disability and poverty: The need for a more nuanced understanding of implications for development policy and practice. *Third World Quarterly, 32*(8), 1493–1513.

Jagger, C., Matthews, R., Melzer, D., Matthews, F., Brayne, C., & MRC CFAS. (2007). Educational differences in the dynamics of disability incidence, recovery and mortality: Findings from the MRC Cognitive Function and Aging Study (MRC CFAS). *International Journal of Epidemiology, 36,* 358–365.

Jenkins, S. P., & Rigg, J. A. (2003). *Disability and disadvantage: Selection, onset, and duration effects* (Institute for Social and Economic Research (ISER) Working Papers Number 2003–18).

Maulik, P. K., & Damstadt, G. L. (2007). Childhood disabilities in low and middle income countries: Overview of screening, prevention, services, legislation and epidemiology. *Pediatrics, 120*(Suppl. 1), S1–S55.

Mauro, V., Biggeri, M., Deepak, S., & Trani, J. F. (2014). The effectiveness of community based rehabilitation programs: An impact evaluation of a quasi-randomised trial. *Journal of Epidemiology and Community Health, 68,* 1102–1108.

Mauro, V., Biggeri, M., & Grilli, L. (2015). Does community based rehabilitation enhance the muldimensional wellbeing of deprived persons with disabilities? A multi-level impact evaluation. *World Development, 76*(C), 190–202.

Mitra, S. (2014). Employment challenges and successes in low- and middle-income countries. In J. Heymann, M. A. Stein, & G. Moreno (Eds.), *Disability and equality at work.* New York: Oxford University Press.

Mitra, S., & Jones, K. (2017). The impact of recent mental health problems on labor supply: New evidence from longitudinal data. *Applied Economics, 49*(1), 96–109.

Mitra, S., Posarac, A., & Vick, B. (2013). Disability and poverty in developing countries: A multidimensional study. *World Development, 41*, 1–18.

Mitra, S., Palmer, M., Kim, H., Mont, D., & Groce, N. (2017). Extra costs of living with a disability: A review and agenda for future research. *Disability and Health*. DOI: http://dx.doi.org/10.1016/j.dhjo.2017.04.007.

Mitra, S., Palmer, M., Mont, D., & Groce, N. (2016). Can households cope with health shocks in Vietnam? *Health Economics, 25*(7), 888–907.

Mizunoya, S. & Mitra, S. (2013). Is there a Disability Gap in Employment Rates in Developing Countries? *World Development, 42*, 28–43.

Mizunoya, S., Mitra, S., & Yamasaki, I. (2016). *Towards inclusive education: The impact of disability on school attendance in developing countries* (Innocenti Working Paper No. 2016-03). Florence: UNICEF Office of Research.

Mont, D., & Cuong, N. (2011). Disability and poverty in Vietnam. *World Bank Economic Review, 25*(2), 323–359.

Rajaratnam, J. K., Marcus, J. R., Levin-Rector, A., et al. (2010). Worldwide mortality in men and women aged 15–59 years from 1970 to 2010: A systematic analysis. *Lancet, 375*, 1704–1720.

Rathod, S. D., Timæus, I. M., Banda, R., et al. (2016). Premature adult mortality in urban Zambia: A repeated population-based crosssectional study. *BMJ Open, 6*, e010801. doi:10.1136/bmjopen-2015-010801.

Santos, I., Sharif, I., Rahman, H. Z., & Zaman, H. (2011). *How do the poor cope with shocks in Bangladesh* (Policy Research Working Paper No. 5810). The World Bank.

Sharma, M. (2007). Evaluation in community based rehabilitation programmes: A strengths, weaknesses, opportunities and threats analysis. *Asia Pacific Disability Rehabilitation Journal, 18*(1), 46.

WHO. (2013). *WHO Global NCD action plan 2013–2020*. Geneva: World Health Organization.

WHO–World Bank. (2011). *World report on disability*. Geneva: World Health Organization.

Yeo, R., & Moore, K. (2003). Including disabled people in poverty reduction work: "Nothing about us, without us". *World Development, 31*(3), 571–590.

CHAPTER 7

Main Results and Implications

Abstract This chapter summarizes the main results of the book. It derives implications for policies and programs, data and research. Overall, this book offers a new understanding and analysis of the links between disability and wellbeing through the human development model and panel data. The book shows that disability needs to be considered from multiple angles including aging, gender, health, and poverty. It also suggests that disability policies are unlikely to be conducive to human development for all if they focus exclusively on changing the environment and are based on an oppressed minority group approach. This book concludes with a call for inclusion *and* prevention interventions as the sustainable solutions to the deprivations associated with impairments and health conditions.

Keywords Disability · Inclusion · Prevention · Washington Group · Africa

JEL I1 · I3 · O15 · O19

This chapter summarizes the main results of this book for each of the four research questions. I then derive implications for policy, data, and further research.

S. Mitra, *Disability, Health and Human Development*,
Palgrave Studies in Disability and International Development,
DOI 10.1057/978-1-137-53638-9_7

7.1 Summary and Some Implications

7.1.1 *How Should Disability Be Defined to Analyze and Inform Policies Related to Wellbeing?*

1. This book introduces the human development model of disability, health, and wellbeing. It is a conceptual framework developed to define disability, describe and explain health deprivations, their causes, and their consequences on wellbeing. The model is based on the capability approach of Amartya Sen and informed by the socioeconomic determinants of health. It defines disability as a deprivation in terms of functionings and/or capabilities among persons with health deprivations (impairment and/or health condition). Health deprivations and disability result from the interaction of personal factors (e.g., sex, age), structural factors (e.g., policies, social attitudes, and physical environment), and resources (e.g., assets, information). It highlights the role of conversion factors and agency in shaping health deprivations and wellbeing. It is universal in that any individual is vulnerable to health deprivations and thus is at risk of disability. It points toward the need for inclusion *and* prevention interventions in health and disability for human development.

The human development model is applied using panel household survey data for Ethiopia, Malawi, Tanzania, and Uganda with the Washington Group short set of questions on six functional difficulties (e.g., seeing, walking) as a measure of health deprivation. The primary focus of the empirical part of the book is descriptive given the scarcity of studies on functional difficulties and wellbeing. Some of the results did vary across countries, while at the same time some patterns emerged, and these patterns for the four countries under study are summarized below. These results dispel some myths around disability when the latter is measured through functional difficulties.

7.1.2 *What Is the Prevalence of Functional Difficulties?*

2. Functional difficulties are not rare among adults in the four countries. The prevalence of functional difficulties (moderate or severe) ranges from 11% in Malawi to 15% in Tanzania and Uganda. The prevalence of severe difficulties is under 2% in Malawi and close to 4% in Ethiopia, Malawi, and Uganda.

These results are consistent with recent findings on prevalence (e.g., WHO–World Bank 2011; Mitra and Sambamoorthi 2014) that dispel the myths that disability is rare and affects a small minority and that disability is an issue pertinent only in the context of HICs.

3. Seeing and walking difficulties are the most common functional difficulties, followed by hearing and concentrating difficulties.

4. A strong age and socioeconomic gradient in the prevalence of functional difficulties is found. About half of individuals 65 or older report functional difficulties. Women are disproportionately more likely to experience difficulties, whatever their age group. Households in the bottom quintile of the asset or expenditure distribution are 1.5–2 times more likely to have a functional difficulty compared to households in the top quintile.

5. Very few persons with functional difficulties use assistive devices (e.g., glasses) or healthcare services that could reduce such difficulties, so some of these difficulties may be preventable. This provides suggestive evidence that poverty may cause functional difficulties, at least in part.

6. Functional difficulties are not static. For Ethiopia and Uganda, where individuals are interviewed twice about their functional difficulties, a lot of persons with functional difficulties at baseline do not report such difficulties a year or two years later, and vice versa. Functional difficulties may change overtime and are fluid. This result dispels the myth that functional difficulties are static or permanent.

7. Individuals experience various degrees of functional difficulties and deprivations. The diversity in the degree of functional difficulties is correlated with the intensity of deprivations. There is not a dichotomous state of disability vs. no disability.

The previous two results imply that we are not referring here to a well-defined minority group, contrary to common perceptions and some of the arguments under the social model and the identity politics approach of the disability rights movement. Persons with functional difficulties are a large and fluid group of people, some with intermittent or temporary difficulties. Some would likely not self-identify as having a disability and may never be connected to disabled people organizations. This point, made earlier (Shakespeare 2014), is supported by the empirical evidence in this book. It is also consistent with the point made by Fujiura (2001) that disability is an ambiguous demographic.

7.1.3 *What Inequalities Are Associated with Functional Difficulties?*

8. There is a significant, consistent, and large association between functional difficulties and deprivations. Among adults, functional difficulties are significantly associated with deprivations in employment, morbidity, and living conditions, economic insecurity and short-term mortality. Functional difficulties are also correlated with multidimensional poverty.

9. While persons with functional difficulties are a disproportionately large share of the poor, not all persons with functional difficulties are poor. Some persons with functional difficulties do achieve levels of well-being comparable to persons with no difficulty. This result dispels the myth that persons with disabilities are always among the poorest of the poor. Having a functional difficulty is not synonymous with being poor but considerably increases the odds of being poor, even in the poorest countries.

These last two results indicate that in Ethiopia, Malawi, Tanzania, and Uganda, persons with functional difficulties often experience deprivations. In a context where most people are poor and where there is little in terms of a social safety net, persons with functional difficulties experience a greater breadth and depth of deprivations than persons without any difficulty. Structural and resource factors contribute to this situation, although this book could not precisely isolate the extent to which structural barriers and resource constraints contribute to deprivations and to functional difficulties.

10. The association between functional difficulties and deprivations varies depending on the trajectory of functional difficulties overtime in Ethiopia and Uganda: Persons with persistent functional difficulties are worse off than persons with a one-time self-report of functional difficulty. Several subgroups are worse off among persons with functional difficulties: older persons, older women, and persons with persistent severe functional difficulties.

11. In all four countries, individuals with functional difficulties have higher odds of mortality within the next two years, everything else held constant. There is a large and consistent association between severe functional difficulties and mortality. There is a smaller but significant association between moderate difficulties and mortality for women and adults younger than 50.

7.1.4 What Are the Economic Consequences of Functional Difficulties?

12. Having increasing functional difficulties is associated with higher odds of leaving work in Ethiopia and Uganda, especially among older adults. It provides suggestive evidence that functional difficulties are a causal factor of poverty through the work channel.

7.2 Implications for Policies and Programs

This book's conceptual framework and empirical findings have several policy implications.

Results on the prevalence of functional difficulties and their association with deprivations show that functional difficulties are relevant to development policy. Disability measured through functional difficulties is indeed highly correlated with deprivations and poverty, whether material or multidimensional. Although Ethiopia, Malawi, Tanzania, and Uganda have national disability policies and legislations and have ratified the CRPD, more policy work is needed to curb the stark inequalities across functional status shown in this book. Current economic systems and societies in the LICs under consideration fail to provide ways to include persons with functional difficulties.

These findings provide ammunitions to demand interventions and policies in the form of the prevention of functional difficulties and the inclusion of persons with functional difficulties. Broadly, education, social protection programs, healthcare coverage, and labor market interventions are policy areas that need to address disability for inequalities to be reduced. In the context of recent calls to 'leave no one behind' in the SDGs, this book shows some of the gaps that need to be closed: 'taking on inequality'[1] requires taking on disability.

The results also show that disability is a crosscutting, not a specialist, issue. The human development model and its application to four countries in Africa show that in policy and research, disability needs to be considered in policies related to aging, health, gender, and poverty.

The findings imply that disability should not be seen as a policy issue that is the luxury of high-income and aging economies.

Functional difficulties seem to be preventable, at least in part, as evidenced by very limited access to assistive devices (e.g., glasses) and healthcare services, pointing toward the need for prevention policies with respect to health conditions/injuries (global health, public health) and functional difficulties (assistive devices, rehabilitation).

Functional difficulties seem to cause poverty, at least via work exits. While accessing work has received attention in the disability and development field, more attention is needed with respect to retaining work following the onset of a functional difficulty.

Overall, these empirical results as well as the human development model suggest that multiple track approaches are needed including at least inclusion and prevention interventions. Disability models and policies that leave out prevention are unlikely to be conducive to human development for all. They do not cover the many people with temporary difficulties or late life onsets who may not self-identify as having a disability and are not connected to disabled people organizations. They also ignore the potential wellbeing enhancements that prevention may bring about.

Despite the recent development of social protection programs in the four countries under study, including cash transfer and public works programs, inequalities across functional difficulty status are stark. The exact impact of social protection programs related to disability needs to be assessed.

More specific policy implications need further analysis at the country level. For instance, on employment policy in the context of Ethiopia, Malawi, Tanzania, and Uganda, with a relatively low employment rate for persons with functional difficulties, one needs to find out why this is the case. It could be due to how the underlying health deprivations reduce the productivity of persons with functional difficulties for the types of jobs that are available. It could be due to a lack of access to assistive devices. It could be due to structural factors, for instance, a physically inaccessible work environment or negative attitudes in the community. Once the main causes for low employment rates are better understood, it becomes feasible to develop evidence-based programs and policies to facilitate employment. The results and data presented in this book show the need for such analysis.

7.3 Implications for Data

Functional difficulty indicators need to become standard in household surveys in LMICs, as well as in the monitoring systems of NGOs and governments, to inform the development of disability-inclusive policies and programs. The use of the Washington Group recommended questions in surveys and monitoring systems would provide some of the necessary data for this monitoring to become feasible across countries.

A measure of functional difficulties should be included as a standard correlate in studies of poverty and economic wellbeing. It would be inconceivable not to include age or gender or marital status variables as correlates. Likewise, applied researchers should at least include a measure such as the Washington Group short set as a potential correlate of poverty. There is also a need to disaggregate poverty statistics such as the $1.90 a day or the MPI and more broadly relevant SDG indicators of the 2030 Agenda for persons with functional difficulties.

More generally, there is a need for internationally produced disability statistics with an academic or an international organization as the scorekeeper. It may have an immense effect on development practice and debates related to disability, health and human development.

More work is needed in terms of disability measurement. For instance, recommendations on the use of the Washington Group questions focus on the group with severe functional difficulties. Analyses should try to incorporate the degree of functional difficulties through different categories or a functional score. Analyses that focus on persons experiencing severe functional difficulties leave out persons with moderate functional difficulties who are at risk of poverty.

In addition, information is lacking considerably and more data is needed on structural factors (e.g., social norms, attitudes, and physical environment) and on health deprivations (e.g., health conditions) that may lead to functional difficulties and/or deprivations. Data collection efforts that collect information on health deprivations such as the Study of Global Aging and Adult Health of WHO and on environmental factors such as the Model Disability Survey (WHO–World Bank 2015) are steps in this direction.

The LSMS data used in this book is rich and yet ripe with limitations for the purpose of this study. It focused on a small set of wellbeing dimensions, often economic in nature. For instance, it had no information on individual subjective wellbeing or on social connections.

Finally, the LSMS data used here could only follow individuals for up to two years. Because of the particularly dynamic nature of functional difficulties during adulthood and the common transitions experienced by adults, it is important to avoid a single point-in-time survey contact and incorporate functional difficulties in longitudinal datasets.

7.4 Further Research

This book has highlighted a number of areas where more research is needed.

The human development model needs to be developed further, and its synergies with the ICF need to be considered. It also needs to be applied with data that captures more aspects of the model, including agency and structural factors (e.g., stigma).

There are puzzles with respect to the links between mortality and functional difficulties: What interventions would prevent onsets, improve recoveries or at least delay their progression to mortality? To what extent are there 'missing persons with disabilities'[2]? In other words, to what extent is the excessive mortality the result of the negative treatment or neglect of persons with disabilities and how can that be stopped?

More research is necessary on dimensions of wellbeing that this study did not have data on, such as subjective wellbeing, political voice and governance, social connections, and relationships.

In addition, qualitative, mixed methods and participatory studies are required to complement the quantitative analysis in this book by trying to understand the results in their complex contexts and by listening to voices and perceptions.

More research is also needed on program or policy evaluations. Social protection programs seem to disproportionately reach persons with functional difficulties in some countries and yet do not appear to manage to do away with inequalities. Some policies and programs that some LMICs have adopted after ratifying the CRPD need to be assessed. Not all such assessments need to be quantitative and large scale in nature. For instance, Díaz Ruiz et al. (2015) do a content analysis of the intentions of a home-based care program in Chile targeted at persons with severe disabilities and find that the program is unlikely to enhance the wellbeing of this group as per the capability approach. This methodology could be used for other policies and programs and is not so resource intensive; it relies primarily on a desk review of policy documents.

Finally, this book's empirical findings were focused on deprivations. Research is needed on successful case studies. The case of Richard who accompanied us throughout Chapters 1 and 2 illustrates this point. Since contracting polio at age six, Richard has had a severe walking difficulty. Richard grew up facing countless challenges associated with poverty and disability. Yet, today, as an adult, Richard does not experience any of the deprivations measured in this study. If not all persons with functional difficulties are poor, and some do achieve levels of wellbeing comparable to persons with no difficulty, it seems key to understand why. Are there personal, structural, or resource factors that helped them maintain or boost their wellbeing and to what extent can these factors work for other people?

Notes

1. 'Taking on Inequality' is in reference to World Bank (2016).
2. This is in reference to 'missing women' in Sen (1990).

References

Díaz Ruiz A., N. Sánchez Durán & A. Palá (2015). *An analysis of the intentions of a Chilean disability policy through the lens of the capability approach.* Journal of Human Development and Capabilities, *6*(4), 483–500.

Fujiura, G. T. (2001). Emerging trends in disability. *Population Today, 29*(6), 9–10.

Mitra, S., & Sambamoorthi, U. (2014). Disability prevalence among adults: Estimates for 54 countries and progress toward a global estimate. *Disability and Rehabilitation, 36*, 940–947.

Sen, A. K. (1990). More than 100 million women are missing. *New York Review of Books*, Dec. 20th, 61–66.

Shakespeare, T. (2014). *Disability rights and wrongs revisited* (2nd ed.). London: Routledge Taylor & Francis.

WHO–World Bank. (2011). *World report on disability.* Geneva: World Health Organization.

WHO–World Bank. (2015). *Model disability survey.* Geneva: World Health Organization. http://www.who.int/disabilities/data/mds/en/. Accessed 14 April 2017.

World Bank. (2016). *Poverty and shared prosperity 2016: Taking on inequality.* Washington, DC: World Bank. doi:10.1596/978-1-4648-0958-3.

Díaz Ruiz A., N. Sánchez Durán & A. Palá (2015). An analysis of the intentions of a Chilean disability policy through the lens of the capability approach. Journal of Human Development and Capabilities, 6(4), 483-500.

Appendices

A.1 Types of functional difficulties among persons with moderate difficulties

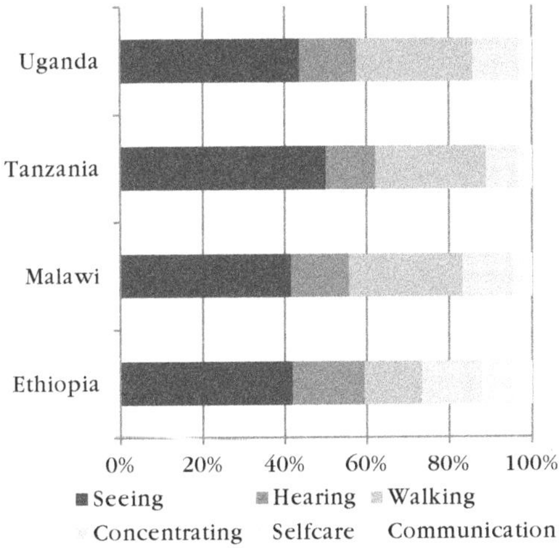

S. Mitra, *Disability, Health and Human Development*,
Palgrave Studies in Disability and International Development,
DOI 10.1057/978-1-137-53638-9

A.2 Types of functional difficulties among persons with moderate and severe difficulties

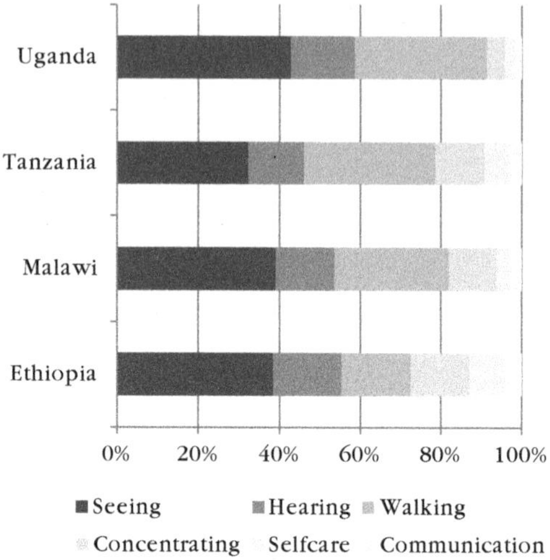

A.3 Prevalence of severe and moderate functional difficulties for the poorest and richest quintiles (%)

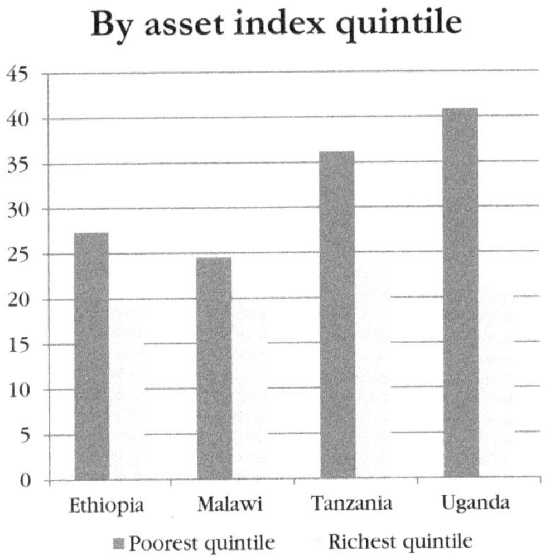

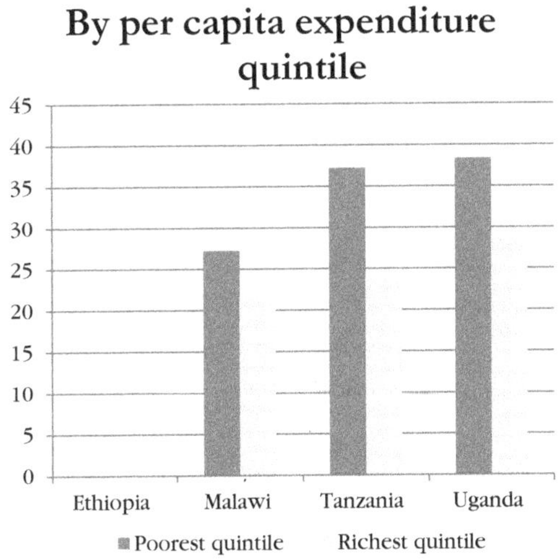

Note Per capita expenditures are not available for Ethiopia

A.4 Multidimensional Poverty Measures by Functional Difficulty Status

	Severe difficulty	Moderate difficulty	No difficulty
H			
Ethiopia	0.89***	0.84***	0.68
Malawi	0.81***	0.68***	0.56
Tanzania	0.94***	0.87***	0.79
Uganda	0.90***	0.71***	0.57
A			
Ethiopia	0.68***	0.60***	0.56
Malawi	0.61***	0.55***	0.51
Tanzania	0.62***	0.55***	0.53
Uganda	0.61***	0.57***	0.53
M_0			
Ethiopia	0.61***	0.51***	0.38
Malawi	0.50***	0.38***	0.28
Tanzania	0.58***	0.48***	0.42
Uganda	0.53***	0.37***	0.21

Notes H, A and M_0 are defined in Box 2. ***indicates significance at 1% level of the difference compared to persons with no difficulty. Statistical significance is tested with *t*-test for A and M_0, Pearson's Chi square test for H

A.5 Multidimensional poverty by functional difficulty status, sex and age group

	Severe	Moderate	None	Severe	Moderate	None
	Women			**Men**		
H						
Ethiopia	0.90***	0.89***	0.73	0.89***	0.79***	0.63
Malawi	0.89***	0.74***	0.62	0.71***	0.61***	0.50
Tanzania	0.95***	0.88***	0.82	0.94***	0.87***	0.75
Uganda	0.96***	0.75***	0.62	0.82***	0.65***	0.52
A						
Ethiopia	0.68***	0.61***	0.58	0.68***	0.59***	0.53
Malawi	0.62***	0.56***	0.52	0.60***	0.54***	0.50
Tanzania	0.63***	0.56***	0.54	0.60***	0.53***	0.52
Uganda	0.62***	0.58***	0.54	0.60***	0.55***	0.52
M_0						
Ethiopia	0.61***	0.54***	0.42	0.61***	0.46***	0.33
Malawi	0.55***	0.41***	0.32	0.42***	0.33***	0.25
Tanzania	0.59***	0.49***	0.44	0.56***	0.46***	0.39
Uganda	0.59***	0.41***	0.25	0.46***	0.32***	0.18
	Persons under age 50			**Persons 50 and older**		
H						
Ethiopia	0.85***	0.80***	0.66	0.92***	0.88***	0.79
Malawi	0.72***	0.60***	0.54	0.87***	0.77***	0.66
Tanzania	0.93***	0.86**	0.79	0.95***	0.89***	0.80
Uganda	0.79***	0.66***	0.57	0.94***	0.80***	0.68
A						
Ethiopia	0.66***	0.58***	0.55	0.69***	0.62***	0.58
Malawi	0.58***	0.53***	0.51	0.63***	0.57***	0.52
Tanzania	0.58***	0.54***	0.53	0.63***	0.55***	0.52
Uganda	0.56***	0.55*	0.50	0.63***	0.58***	0.53
M_0						
Ethiopia	0.56***	0.46***	0.37	0.63***	0.55***	0.46
Malawi	0.42***	0.32***	0.28	0.55***	0.44***	0.34
Tanzania	0.54***	0.47***	0.42	0.60***	0.49***	0.42
Uganda	0.43***	0.36***	0.24	0.59***	0.44***	0.33

Notes H, A and M_0 are defined in Box 2. Estimates are weighted. ***, ** and * indicates significance at 1%, 5% and 10% levels respectively of the difference compared to persons with no difficulty. Statistical significance is tested with t-test for A and M_0, Pearson's Chi square test for H

A.6 Regression of the adjusted multidimensional poverty headcount (M_0)

	Ethiopia	Malawi	Tanzania	Uganda
Functional score	0.37***	0.55***	0.34***	0.24***
Personal factors				
Age 15–39 (reference)				
Age 40–49	0.04***	0.02***	−0.02	0.03**
Age 50–64	0.09***	0.05***	0.00	0.06***
Age 65+	0.14***	0.12***	0.08***	0.19***
Male	−0.09***	−0.08***	−0.04***	−0.09***
Resources				
Mother had no schooling	0.09***	0.10***	0.03***	NA***
Structural factors				
Household				
Married	0.02***	−0.02***	−0.05***	0.03***
Household head	0.00	−0.01*	−0.04***	0.02*
Household size	0.00	0.00**	0.00	−0.01***
Community				
Distance to healthcare services	0.00*	0.00*	0.00***	0.00***
Rural	0.16***	0.14***	0.02**	0.08**
Constant	0.15***	0.13***	0.43***	0.22***

Notes Table includes coefficients of all independent variables in a multivariate regression of the adjusted multidimensional headcount M_0. ***, **, * indicate significance at 1, 5, and 10% levels. Mother's schooling is not available for Uganda

A.7 Odds Ratio of Being Deprived in Each Dimension by Functional Difficulty Type

	Ethiopia	Malawi	Tanzania	Uganda
Having less than primary school completion				
Seeing	0.84	0.74***	1.04	0.82*
Hearing	1.64*	1.51***	1.05	1.63***
Walking	1.48*	1.36***	2.95***	1.59***
Concentrating	1.72*	1.07	1.45	1.53**
Communication	1.18	1.38	2.7	1.82*
Selfcare	0.85	2.09**	0.59	4.45***
Being sick or injured recently				
Seeing	2.01***	1.56***	1.06	1.53***
Hearing	1.32**	1.22*	1.31	1.15
Walking	2.42***	2.29***	1.59***	1.66***
Concentrating	2.03***	1.46***	0.61*	1.38*
Communication	1.28	0.86	0.51	0.93
Selfcare	0.57**	1.45*	1.70	1.08
Not working				
Seeing	1.22**	1.17**	1.45***	1.33**
Hearing	1.15	1.3**	1.07	1
Walking	1.24*	1.78***	1.93***	2.21***
Concentrating	1.56***	1.49***	3.01***	1.87***
Communication	0.99	0.94	2.31*	2.27***
Selfcare	1.41*	3.78***	13.21***	9.07***
Being materially deprived				
Seeing	1.1	0.85**	0.83	0.97
Hearing	1.59	1.85***	1.18	1.57**
Walking	2.31*	1.2*	1.3	1.33**
Concentrating	0.95	0.84	1.19	1.01
Communication	1	1.43	4.38	0.72
Selfcare	0.76	1.02	0.89	0.94
Being economically insecure				
Seeing	1.2**	1.04	3.74***	1.34***
Hearing	1.12	1.44***	0.74	1.28*
Walking	1.05	1.34***	1.19	1.39***
Concentrating	1.26	1.44**	0.82	1.52***
Communication	0.98	0.79	1.13	0.54**
Selfcare	0.97	1.02	1.45	1.14

Notes For each country, results show the estimated odds ratio of being deprived in one dimension (e.g. not working) for each functional difficulty (e.g. seeing) compared to a person without such functional difficulty in the entire sample of adults. All regressions are run as logistic regressions. Coefficients are odds ratios. ***significant at the 1% level, **significant at the 5% level, *significant at the 10% level. More information on the dependent variables is in Table 5.2. The regression controls are as follows: age categories, sex, being married, being the household head, having a mother with no prior schooling, household size and distance to healthcare

A.8 Descriptive Statistics for All Adults by Mortality Status Within Two Years

	Ethiopia		Malawi		Tanzania		Uganda	
	All	Died	All	Died	All	Died	All	Died
Moderate functional difficulty	0.09	0.17**	0.10	0.18***	0.09	0.15***	0.12	0.23***
Severe functional difficulty	0.03	0.27***	0.01	0.05***	0.04	0.21***	0.04	0.28***
Functional limitation score	0.01	0.10***	0.01	0.03***	0.18	0.10***	0.02	0.09***
	(0.00)	(0.02)	(0.00)	(0.01)	(0.00)	(0.02)	(0.00)	(0.13)
Personal factors								
Age	34.48	53.64***	34.15	52.93***	34.72	53.73***	33.31	57.98***
	(0.24)	(2.79)	(0.22)	(1.83)	(0.19)	(2.08)	(0.23)	(2.50)
Male	0.50	0.60***	0.43	0.54	0.48	0.53	0.49	0.58
Resources								
Mother had no schooling[1]	NA	NA	0.92	0.93*	0.59	0.80***	NA	NA
Structural factors								
Household								
Married	0.63	0.74***	0.62	0.64	0.40	0.44	0.49	0.49
Household head	0.38	0.55***	0.41	0.61***	0.35	0.52***	0.34	0.51***
Household size	5.72	5.21**	5.54	4.98***	3.85	4.17	8.46	7.86
	(0.03)	(0.29)	(0.03)	(0.19)	(0.02)	(0.23)	(0.08)	(0.50)
Community								
Distance to healthcare	15.30	17.49	22.23	22.79	5.76	5.30	25.51	21.93
	(0.21)	(1.90)	(0.39)	(0.75)	(0.13)	(0.77)	(0.54)	(24.8)
Rural	0.99	0.99	0.73	0.70	0.71	0.73	0.78	0.84

Sources Author's calculations using Ethiopia Rural Socioeconomic Survey (2011/12, 2013/2014), Malawi Integrated Household Survey (2010/2011, 2012/2013), Tanzania National Panel Survey (2010/2011, 2012/2013) and Uganda National Panel Survey (2009/2010, 2011). *Notes* Estimates are weighted

[1]Mother's schooling, data is not available for a large share of the sample in Uganda and in Ethiopia for the initial wave

A.9 ODDS RATIO OF SHORT-TERM DEATH AND SEVERE FUNCTIONAL DIFFICULTY TYPES

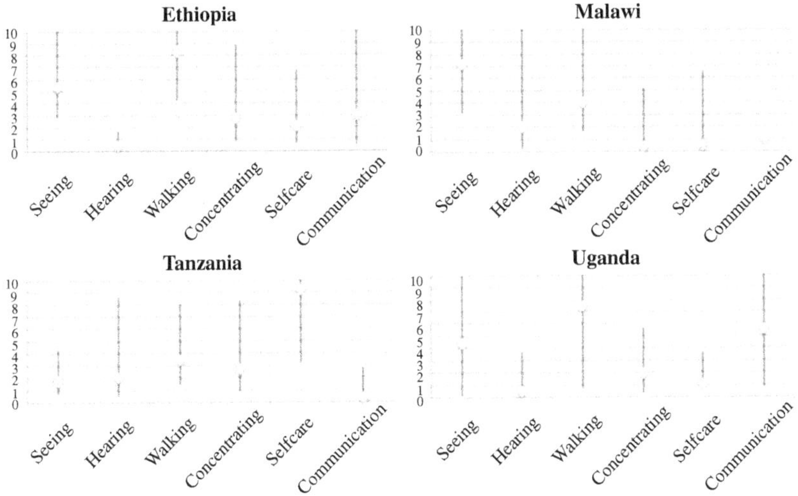

Index

S. Mitra, *Disability, Health and Human Development*,
Palgrave Studies in Disability and International Development,
DOI 10.1057/978-1-137-53638-9

CPSIA information can be obtained
at www.ICGtesting.com
Printed in the USA
LVHW072228181119
637806LV00019B/182/P

9 781137 536372